2.0

inside of me

MY STORY.

WITH A 20-YEAR LENS.

SHELLIE R. WARREN

INSIDE OF ME 2.0
My Story. With a 20-Year Lens.

Library of Congress Control Number: 2024945105

ISBN (paperback): 9781662941726
eISBN: 9781662941733

Table of Contents

Dedication

I actually didn't plan on dedicating this book to anyone at first. However, once it was finished and I felt a full release, I then thought about how so many individuals who were around for *Inside of Me* have passed on since. As faces and names ran through my mind, there were certain ones who, without question, saw me, affirmed me, *believed me*, validated and celebrated me in ways very few ever have. I want to acknowledge them for that: Carolyn Demonbreun, Janice Chaffee, Marcus Jordan, Sarah Gaines, Jerome Brown and Chuck Stanford. Throughout the years, we understood our unique kind of friendship and the special and sacred purpose behind it. Thank you for the signature seeds planted because they continue to thrive which means that your spirit continues to flourish. "You are missed" is such an understatement. Continue to get your well-deserved rest. You've earned it.

And to the spirit of Perez. Perez is a book of its own. For now, I'll just say that you should check out the Message Version of Romans 8 at some point because there are a lot of ways to be pregnant. Through the spirit of Perez — something that the Spirit spoke into my life and world several years ago — I have experienced breakthroughs, after breakthroughs, after breakthroughs; that is just what Perez means, so...it tracks. That said, please learn how to not see things one-dimensionally. Watch how it totally changes your life once you do. Perez, for being a part of me, daily, I thank you too.

> *"Only a few people care.*
> *The rest are just nosy."*
>
> (UNKNOWN)

Foreword

Several years back, when I took a spiritual gifts test (if you don't know what that is, it's gifts that the Bible says will edify the Church—meaning other people; I Corinthians 12 is the reference), I decided to do some research into the pros and cons of having particular ones (yes, there is such a thing). One of my top gifts is wisdom and, from what I've learned, a trait that comes with having that is saying things like, "God said" or "God told me". Apparently, only those with the gift feel confident enough to be so bold. Hmph. Maybe that's why I can say, with complete peace and total ease, that when I was 12, GOD TOLD ME something that now, at almost 50 (at the time of writing this—my birthday is June 17, 1974), has proven to be quite true: "Your heart will be broken often and your health will remain intact."

CHILE.

What's really wild about both of those things is plenty of people in my family have health-related issues, not just physical but mental health too, including my father who took his life three months before I turned 40 and two of my uncles who did the same years prior. Me? I'm rarely sick. Oh, but that brokenhearted thing? *Listen.* And as I sat down to pen this sequel to my first book, I believe the reason why a broken heart, sometimes on-loop, is the "thorn in my flesh" so to speak, is because God didn't tell me out of nowhere that my heart and health would play out in certain ways. No, it came after I declared, at

12, that I was going to be a generational curse breaker in my family— and boy, is there a lot of BS to clear out of my bloodline. SMDH.

And so now, 20 years later, with "20" biblically meaning "perfection in waiting", I get that book number one, *Inside of Me: Lessons of Lust, Love and Redemption*, was about addressing certain battles that I had within me as a direct result of there being so many curses, strongholds and, quite frankly, conscious poor decisions from so many who came before me, while *Inside of Me. 2.0* is about revealing the specifics of what some of those things actually were.

Now, I will say this: Anyone who knows me knows that I don't tap dance around stuff. The Good Book says that the truth will make us free and disciples walk in truth (John 8:31-32). Therefore, on some levels, we're about to "go there" because covering up things, deflecting, avoiding personal accountability— shoot, flat-out lying, that is why so much mess is all up and in our family trees as it is.

I will also say this: No matter what I do say in this offering, I am being intentional *and* merciful because so much more could be said — and the people who know that I'm talking about them, they know this to be true. Words cannot express how it has always been so wild to me that victims of other folks' selfishness, toxicity and sometimes pure delusional behavior are only further victimized by trying to cover up the harm that was done to them so that the victimizers won't further "suffer". Anyway, certain people who I know are only reading this book to see how much about them is revealed in order to protect their image, brand or even the lies they've told others and themselves so that they can sleep better at night, again— mercy is abundant. Regardless of what I say, I intentionally held back and mercy has flowed freely. Give thanks.

I will also say this: I do believe in God, Christ and the Holy Spirit. I am not a Christian, though; I like the word "disciple" *far more* because I know the origin story of both. I have been studying Hebrew culture for years now, so the westernized watered-down version of "belief", I do not subscribe to. This means that those of you who may gasp at Scripture sometimes being used *and* cuss words as well — well, I know (for instance) that "OMG", which I hear Christians say incessantly, is taking the Lord's name in vain, which is breaking a commandment (the third one, to be exact — Exodus 20:7). I'm also aware that profanity actually means "irreverence for God and sacred things" not saying "damn" or "hell"; not to mention the fact that cuss words actually originate from taboo topics that were turned into slang terms that people now call "cussing" (so many of y'all don't even know why you do or don't do what you do...or don't do) — I address taboo stuff...A LOT, so that also tracks. Adding to that, since a lot of y'all like to be pagan (even though the Bible speaks against that) and will justify skirting around clear biblical instructions like honoring the true Sabbath (Exodus 20:8-11) or learning what adultery actually is (which isn't infidelity; it's marrying someone else while your former spouse is still alive—Matthew 19:1-12, I Corinthians 7:10-11) or observing holidays over holy days — I'm not interested in any of your commentary or faux shock. The American Church is a walking contradiction on a billion different levels when it comes to hypocrisy and cherry-picking the Word, so...I'm good on what you think you have to impart. I grew up in one of the most pompous denominations there is and it about destroyed me. Please spare me the rhetoric.

You know, one of my favorite quotes of all-time is by educator Richard Halverson who once said, "When the Greeks got the Gospel, they turned it into a philosophy; when the Romans got it, they turned it into a government; when the Europeans got it, they turned it into a culture; and when the Americans got it, they turned it into a business." To that, I know what true religion is defined as in Scripture: taking care of widows and orphans and not allowing the world to jack you up (James 1:27) — and honestly, some of the most worldly people around (as far as manipulating Scripture to justify nonsense) are the modern-day Pharisees known as "church folks". Back in the day, the Pharisees plotted to kill Christ (Matthew 12:14) because they were too arrogant and ridiculous to recognize him; today, their descendants are also too arrogant and ridiculous to realize who *really* is about "their Father's business" vs. just doing cyclic...church stuff. I see that for what it is. I am writing all of this with that very point in mind.

Bottom line, my first book had a Christian publisher and I still had some fears that I simply don't anymore. I'm not 29 writing my first book; I'm 49 writing my third. Twenty years have passed and a lot of life and revelations about life have transpired. I found a publishing route that will complement all of this.

That said, if you're reading this offering just to be nosy or messy, you're grown, do you. What I will say is you won't get nearly as much out of it as if you're reading to learn about how I survived so much in hopes that you can avoid some of your own pitfalls along the way and/ or gain the courage that you need in order to "confess and be healed" — because that is also biblical (James 5:16).

Again, you're grown, so you can do whatever you wish; that's a given.

I do hope that you'll choose wisely, though. Time is too precious not to.

Now, let's get into it.

No Acknowledgments? That IS an Acknowledgment.

Anyone who knows me (and only I get to determine who that is...some of y'all will catch that later) knows that it's pretty on-brand for me to not do things the typical or predictable way. So, while I know that it is customary to have acknowledgments at the beginning of a book and while I actually did have them in my first two books, I've decided to go without them this go 'round (I didn't want endorsements either; no need).

There are a few reasons why.

One reason is because one of the many things that hindsight has taught me is people can be very nosy — aggressively and invasively so. They want to see who you claim to be connected to and even how things may have shifted from read to read. Here's the thing, though: At the end of the day, it's really no one's business but my own who I consider to be my tribe, my safe spaces and my support system. Besides, if there's one thing that I do, that my crew can certainly vouch for, it's give. They know they're appreciated. There's no need for an Instagram-post-in-the-form-of-a-published-book-liner for them to feel it. I got them.

Another reason is because I'm going to cover quite a bit of ground on certain issues and while my mission is to share the truth of what transpired, my goal isn't to humiliate anyone (I'm gonna do my best; we'll see what happens). And the reality is that many people who I once considered to be a friend or a close character in the play of my life, they simply aren't anymore. If their names are missing from the acknowledgments, the nosy folks who I was just referring to could easily connect some dots…and them creating their own distorted picture is not what I'm setting out to do.

Still one more reason is, my people know that as other milestones happen over this life journey of mine, I'm not interested in a lot of my folks meetin'-and-greetin'. If God wants y'all to meet, he'll handle it. Otherwise — no over-the-top birthday parties. No big wedding. I don't even want a funeral. My trusted folks know what to do in all of those scenarios. This one? It's partly because I'm ambivert. Partly because it's a signature Shellie move. And it's also because I can't tell you how many times random folks have taken it upon themselves to attempt to connect themselves to certain people, simply on the strength of my connection with them. Listen, one of my favorite verses in Scripture is John 6:70, where Christ said that he's chosen his disciples — and his devil. I used to "choose devils"; I don't anymore. Whatever I can do to keep wolves who look like sheep from out of my space, that is just what I'm going to do. Betrayal is not an interest of mine. Been past that mountain more than enough, chile.

And finally, if I were to even attempt to thank my safe spaces for all that they've done for me since the season that they've entered into my life, they each would probably be getting their own book-length statements; that's how valuable they are to me.

So, no names. Sorry not sorry.

The ones who are the real ones, we've got a billion more memories to make.

For now, for holding me down, even in the support of all of what I'm about to say, I love you. Thank you. Times infinity. Truly.

"We are healed of suffering, only by
experiencing it to the full."
(MARCEL PROUST)

Chapter One

Separating "PTSD Shellie" from the REAL Shellie

Whenever I share a quote or resolve that I find to be profound, I try and give credit to the source. And so, when it comes to what I'm about to say, it comes from a woman named Sandy BeCoats. I haven't spoken to Sandy in years; however, back in the day, I would sometimes visit her church when she was scheduled to speak (I originally met her because she was a supervisor at one of my last "corporate" gigs back in the day). Anyway, as far as her messages went, there are two things she said that always stayed with me. One is that she used to sneak around and spend money behind her husband's back; she called that "financial infidelity" (she's right; it is). You know, a lot of divorces transpire due to financial stress and strain. I wonder how many people are willing to own that it's largely due to their financial unfaithfulness. Moving on, another thing about marriage that Sandy shared is the fact that one of the biggest problems within that type of relational dynamic is the fact that far too many men are married to "Eve" and not "the Woman".

Listen. Here.

If you don't get where she's coming from with that, what she was basically saying is, the Woman was Adam's wife's name in the Garden of Eden, prior to sin (Genesis 2:23), while Eve is the name that

Adam gave her after sin took place (Genesis 3:20). Now, before getting deeper into this, let me just put it right on out there that I am not a feminist on any level (other than supporting that women should get equal work for equal pay). Yeah, some of y'all need to look up the agenda of the likes of women like Margaret Sanger, Gloria Steinem and Dorothy Pittman Hughes, especially as it relates to what they sought to do to the Black family and community. After doing that, spend time in the Word and tell me what about it, especially within modern-day feminism, sounds Scripturally sound (yeah, I'll wait).

No, what I am is a complementarian. Those are basically individuals who believe that, in the eyes of God, men and women's value are *equal,* although our purposes are quite *different*; the differences are beautiful because masculinity and femininity create a balance and balance is good. OK, so since I choose to see things through this type of lens, that is why it is ridiculous to me that some women are all up in their feelings about things like when a man calls his lady "My Woman" as they pontificate (or is it ramble on?) about how women are not property (even though social media has made an entire platform out of "my man, my man, my man"). *Is that not the same thing that Adam said when he first saw his own bride?* Feminism has so many of y'all thinking that you are being empowered when, actually, you're being hustled out of your own biblical birthrights. I'm not gonna debate it either. The West perverts most things about the East and its culture and, contrary to what these evangelicals have so many of you out here thinking, *the Bible is Eastern-cultured.*

Aight, so what does all of this have to do with this particular chapter, especially its title? Well, Sandy was right on it when she said that Adam going from "my Woman" to "Eve" automatically spoke to a breakdown in his connection with his wife, whether folks choose to see it or not. Yeah, as my mother says when she hears insightful things, "Flesh and blood did not reveal that to her" and, honestly, that revelation needs to be preached a whole lot more. Women, as wives, definitely need to ponder more if they are living as if they are a part of their husband ("bone of my bone and flesh of my flesh") or if they are somewhere talking to other spirits and doing what they think is right over what they've already been instructed, by God and his Word, regarding what is best (including when it comes to submission. By the way, husbands and wives DO NOT "submit to each other"; that is not how submission works. Ephesians 5 speaks of husbands submitting to Christ and wives submitting to their husband. If husbands were to submit to their wife, why doesn't Genesis 3:16, Colossians 3:18, I Peter 3:1-17 and Titus 2:5 speak on that? Let's not manipulate Scripture because parts of it are uncomfortable).

And *that* is what brings me to another revelation from the Garden of Eden: although so many folks think that the biggest issue was what transpired between Adam and the Woman, it's *actually* what went down between the Woman and the serpent. If you go back and read Genesis 3, as the serpent was engaging the Woman, he didn't bring up Adam or the Woman's relationship with him one time. No, where he tripped the Woman up was by telling her that God was holding out on her by not allowing her to eat of the tree because it would make her like God — and *that* is what got her, hook, line and sinker. *The Woman took the fruit because the Woman wanted to be like God; she wanted to "get on his level".*

There is real time to get into all of this yet that is what Luciferians are on; they don't have "a problem" with God, it's just that they think they *are* gods — you know, similar to how Lucifer once said that "I will be like the Most High" (Isaiah 14:14). In their minds, they and God are peers. Shoot, and while we're here, even Satanists come to mind. I've had conversations with Satanists before (fear them for what? I have God on my side) and they have told me that, although they have "denominations" similar to how Christianity does, most of them don't seek to actually worship Satan himself (at least, not from their perspective); *who they worship is self*. Goodness. When they told me that, do you know what my immediate response to hearing that was? "Oh…so a lot of Christians are actually Satanists and don't even know it, huh?" to which one of them laughed and said, "You just might be on to something there."

Hosea 4:6 tells us that people perish for a lack of knowledge. Perish doesn't just mean to die. It also means to suffer destruction, ruin and to go through a sort of spiritual death. This means that you can be physically living and yet spiritually be a dead man (or woman) walking. And sadly, because far too many people choose to play "the gossip game" when it comes to spirituality, they are out here going off of what their denomination says (no questions asked) or some popular pastor "preaches" (Luke 6:26 tells us that our task is to be true, not popular) or whatever movement gets the most social media attention at the time.

And *that's* probably why (for example) most folks have never even thought about the fact that a huge part of the reason why women think that men are to hunt and chase them (where is that in Scripture? Adam was a gardener, a cultivator, not a hunter and the Woman was actually *brought* to him; he didn't pursue her — Genesis 2:22). It's also why they have no issue with saying egomaniacal things like they are goddesses, they should be worshipped, men should be obsessed with them and they deserve the princess treatment (umm, princesses are daughters of fathers; queens are wives of kings…grown-acting women deserve kings and queens aren't coddled like little children). This and all of the other god-complex dating and relationship nonsense is because many of them have an "Eve" mentality and not a TRUE WOMAN one.

They are moving around as the PTSD version of the Woman, not the original one. Sadly, folks don't know how to date or court because of it and marriages are suffering because of it. People are justifying doing what the Word says that God hates (divorce — Malachi 2:14-16), multiple times in fact, because of it.

And Christians? Because they are so busy thinking that they are "little Christs" who only need to teach others and not be taught anything, because, in their minds, they already have "the truth" (how is that the case when most of them can't even get on the same page about something as basic as Sabbath-keeping? Ridiculous) — many basically have the mind of a Satanist because they are caught up in their egos instead of humbling themselves to realize that they have so much more about God — and the Godhead overall (I say Godhead because you know that trinity is not in the Bible, right? I John 5:8) — to learn...because that's just how vast God is. Yet nooooo...they are walking around as the PTSD version of a Christian instead of seeking to learn (got to be humble to learn something — Proverbs 22:4) how to be a true disciple...which is what Christ himself called his followers to be.

And why are so many women doing this? Why are so many Christians doing this as well? My belief is because it's more comfortable to do what the masses are doing (even though Scripture absolutely instructs us to not follow "the wide gate" — Matthew 7:13-14). Hmph. Kind of like how James 5:16 tells us that with confession comes healing. Meanwhile, look at how many lies, deflections, selective memories church folks — from the leadership on down — tend to have. CONFESS AND BE HEALED is the spiritual prescription, not DEFLECT AND HOPE FOR THE BEST. And honestly, that's just one more form of PTSD that so many Christians are dealing with — they can't ever get to the real version of themselves because they don't tell the truth about who they (currently) are and why they do so many of the things that they do. Because they are looking from the eyes of unhealed trauma, they think that so long as they slap on a Scripture (oftentimes, a totally out of context one), they can move past their habits, secrets, issues and weaknesses.

Me? I'm not that kind of person. I never really have been. Although, I do think that there is a difference between being private and sneaky and that there is indeed a place for privacy, I don't give anyone enough power in my life to be afraid to confess so that I can be healed — so that "PTSD Shellie" can be put out of her misery and REAL Shellie can finally live in a state of peace, freedom and full transparency. Yeah, I spent some years "entertaining serpents" which caused me to be a "version" of myself. I don't do that anymore. I am free.

Honestly, that's a lot of what this book is all about. Twenty years from when I wrote my first one, one that consisted of quite a bit of confessing, it is now time to connect some dots in order to understand how I got to a place of healing — and no, it wasn't easy. Some days, it was excruciating as hell. Oh, but as the late philosopher Thomas Hobbes once said, "Hell is truth seen too late." In other words, hell is when you avoid the truth...not when you actually face it.

So, with all of this in mind, let me just say that this is a very frank, candid and "oh well" kind of offering. At 50 (by the time this book is officially published), now more than ever, I don't have or make time to mince words or try and figure out how to make people feel comfortable with my own story, experiences and testimony. And because this is how I get down, I'm pretty sure that you're going to have moments when you will be like, "Well damn, Shellie" and I'm more than fine with that. The individuals in my life who have actually invested in REAL Shellie (and again, only I would know who those individuals are), they all have encouraged, supported and given me their blessing to proceed.

Their prayers have me covered. I'm not concerned about those who choose to *prey* instead of *pray*. I'm used to your type. I couldn't be more over you.

Also, let me give the heads up now that, although there will be times when things will seem harsh, dark, and definitely super awkward — perhaps even to the point of feeling a bit afflictive, especially if you know that I'm talking about you and some of you will indeed pick up on that very vibe — there is a method to the madness. With me, there always is.

See, in the first book, although I was just as *forthcoming*, I still had quite a bit of fear because I was still attached to people who were trying to keep me under their control by using fear as a tactic and stratagem. Oh, but as the Good Book says, "*there* is no fear in love" and "perfect love casts out fear" (I John 4:18). And so, now that those individuals are released (I choose to release people rather than "cut them off"; it's kinder), there's a lot less post-traumatic stress going on and a whole lot more "This is the core of who I am — deal with it or don't" along with an Elmo shrug that comes from the very depths of my soul.

Y'all, there is something very fascinating about folks who are able to get truly real — as they find freedom, all of the fake folks find new persons, places, things and ideas to manipulate. Ah yes, in the wise words of Tupac Shakur, "The realest people don't have a lot of friends." Guess what? We don't want them either. Anything or anyone who would require us to be a shell, façade or "version" of ourselves over the way that we were created to be before life came and "life-d us" — they aren't genuine friends anyway. Listen, anyone who doesn't want you to be the *real* you? They are a form of trauma in your life.

And with that said, let's go deeper, knowing that, as much as I possibly could, you've been prepared (or warned) for all that comes next.

*"Spiritual narcissists hit hard.
They devastate your belief, soul and life —
and do it under the most manipulative
guise of healing you."*
(MELANIE TONIA EVANS)

Chapter Two

Let's Talk About Church-Related Narcissistic Abuse for a Sec, Shall We?

I ain't got no lies to tell you; my writing process is somewhat of an interesting one. In fact, my mother has always called me her "signs and wonders" child (sometimes from a place of experiencing impromptu "ah ha" moments, other times from being low-key annoyed; I can always tell the difference based on the context of when and how she said it) and that would definitely be the case when it comes to how I move as a writer. Sometimes, I'll know something that I want to write about, yet I won't feel comfortable about penning it until I get a sign. I never know where it's gonna come from either; all I know is that it will arrive right when it's time for me to proceed.

For this particular chapter, it came while I was in the mall where I minister (ministry is service and there's a particular mall in Nashville where I find myself doing that, quite a bit). It's also where, over the last holiday season (prior to releasing this), I simply went to get myself a steak — or so I thought. While walking in, I ran into someone who I hadn't seen in well over a decade. I've always loved her; liked her too. It's just that, when it comes to friendship, there are "levels to this thing" and basically, I enjoy us ...running into each other, catching up and then doing it again whenever the universe causes it to happen. It's a part of our charm.

Anyway, as we were both trying to give each other the *Reader's Digest* version of our lives over the past 10 years, yet again, when the topic of church and church attendance came up and I shared that I had graduated from Adventism and Christianity (I got that phrasing from a dear friend of mine who said that when he attends church, he sees it like going to his alma mater on Homecoming Weekend; still fond memories. It's just that he's moved on), she said that she was pretty much flipping between two Adventist churches herself. Then she casually said two things that let me know that, yep — it's time to tackle this topic head-on.

The Church is dying. That is obvious.

So many people had a problem with your first book. They thought you were lying about "him".

Le sigh. The more things change, the more they absolutely don't at all. So, here's the deal: I haven't been a member of any church for well over 17 years now and I don't have one regret about it. I have learned more about the Bible since leaving. I have pivoted into Hebrew culture (which helps me to understand the Bible better) since leaving. I have been mentally, emotionally and relationally (including sexually) healthier and safer since leaving (ain't that a wild thing to say?). I've had more peace since leaving, especially when it comes to Adventism. And I know it's because a lot of it is tied to spiritual narcissism, which is a very real thing — both in Adventism and in Christianity overall — especially in this country.

I'll tackle Adventism first — for now. I mean, how could a denomination that stands ten toes down that they have "the truth" as they carry such a patronizing and condescending tone that everyone is wrong but them not be narcissistic on some level? And if you've never considered the fact that spiritual narcissism is quite real, by definition: people who talk more than they listen; people who are unteachable; people who manipulate or weaponize Scripture for the sake of their own agenda and purposes; people who "level others" (think of the Pharisees of Christ's time); people who will do whatever they need to do to cover up their own mistakes, offenses and even immoral and illegal activity in order to protect their "brand" (yeah, really bookmark that one) — people who walk around acting like they sit at the right hand of God himself? These are all textbook signs of being a spiritual narcissist. And growing up, I was among the cream of the crop of them, pretty much anywhere I went, including at school and in church.

Y'all, when I look back on my Adventism experience, there are a ton of folks who I know thought they were the complete and total ish. Mercy (literally), don't give a gifted person a mic and a platform on the pulpit; if there is no humility there, you are literally feeding a monster. Case in point, when the news came out about me being molested, for years, I remember coming home one day to a pastor — A PASTOR — who was my mom's friend, who I was never a fan of, telling me what the game plan was going to be. Here I was, 15, and no one asked me what *I thought* needed to be done about *my being violated*. Nope, the man who hurt and harmed me was basically an Adventist celebrity, so they came up with a strategy that was best to/for them — and for him. Not only that but folks had the nerve to be so caught up in their narrative of him that, to this day, many of them choose to (attempt to) revictimize me by either flat-out saying or not-so-subtly implying that I made my abuse up...yep, right to my face. *Why would a child make up such a thing? How toxic are y'all?*

Yet I have to remember that this approach is on-brand for oh so many of them. Another example is an Adventist teenager I once went to school with who used to babysit some kids for a married couple for years while the husband was at home. She ended up becoming his child mistress and while she got ostracized for it, ask me if he ever went to jail — oh, my bad...*prison*? From what I hear, he's actually a pastor now and, last that she and I talked, she still hates coming back to Nashville to this day. A child is the victim of statutory rape and, in response, the churches around here acted like she needed a scarlet letter on all of her coats or something

Another example: A man who went to the church that I grew up in, the rumors about him and multiple women never seemed to cease and yet nothing was done about it. I mean, he was a great music leader, so let's overlook all of the crazy. Thankfully, I was never a victim at his hands personally — although, indirectly, one of his daughters was the worst "friend" I've had in history (she was Nellie Olsen in my first book) and that sent me on the course for not choosing other female friends very wisely, not to mention the fact that her abortion referrals ultimately resulted in me not having someone to carry on my father's bloodline after I die. Bad girlfriends? They are the absolute worst. On a billion different levels.

Still another: When I was sexually assaulted at an Adventist high school (an institution where I witnessed some of the most mind-blowing racist situations too; the EEOC really should have shut that school down back in the 90s) by one Black teen and one white teen, my mother actually told me it was my fault, while the school refused to press charges because of how it would look. One of the faculty members literally told me to keep it under wraps. What's wildly disgusting about that is I was told that the Black guy actually ended up sexually assaulting other women later down the road.

And because plenty of narcissism and so little accountability are basically the tagline for both my church experiences and observations throughout the years, my molester would *still feel* like he had the right to speak to me, try to hug me (*are you nuts?*) and even, just a few years ago, send me an email (that *my mother* gave him access to — both of them are still Adventists, by the way) all the while acting like he was somehow doing me a favor by leaving me alone prior to my receiving it. I promise you that it's rare when I'm totally rendered speechless yet I 1,000 percent was as I watched this man try to give me instructions on how to handle a family matter with someone who wasn't even his own relative. *Dude, are you insane?* Perhaps. However, more than anything, you belong to a denomination that is full of narcissism — so, of course, clearly, you feel so supremely superior that you would have the right to still dictate thoughts and actions to someone you once harmed, when you really should just mind your own business and be thankful, daily, that they never put you up underneath a prison somewhere. For years, I've told you to leave me alone. LEAVE. ME. ALONE.

And before some of y'all even start, you can forgive someone and set firm boundaries at the same time. Know who doesn't believe that? NARCISSISTS. Don't believe me? Google it. There is plenty of information out here, by mental health experts, who support that narcissists don't like the word "no". They don't want people to set limits for them and they can't even fathom not having access to whatever you have that they want...because, in life, narcissists make everything about them. And so, they see boundaries as a personal attack.

OK, so back to the church-related stuff...

Oh, but Shellie, how can you put all of that on just one denomination? Trust me, chile, I absolutely am not. I'm merely speaking of my own experience with the one that *I* grew up in. Please don't think it's escaped me that others have the same ridiculous reputation (Church of Christ and COGIC immediately come to mind). In fact, sadly, when I went through a season of seeking more truth via other churches (and denominations), I encountered some next-level spiritual narcissists (especially in leadership) from the places that I visited/attended as well — ones that had the Jezebel spirit and even some straight-up witchcraft attached to them.

How do I know? Because I don't just throw words like that around. Contrary to what a lot of church folks do, I am very intentional about studying more than emotionalizing things. Therefore, I know what comes with the Jezebel spirit too: control; manipulation; selfishness; pride; the constant need for attention; operating from a false sense of humility; constantly doing harm and then deflecting by playing the victim; picking on the weak and ostracizing the strong (because when Jezebels can't manipulate you, they see no use for you); seeking out the wounded because it makes them feel good about themselves to "heal" them — always acting "super-spiritual". And, as far as witchcraft goes, some very telling signs of it being in the Church is when people manipulate Scripture to fit their own agenda; they think everyone who doesn't do just what they say are being rebellious (because they think people should *serve them* more than *obey God* and that is due to their own god-complex) and they take "the hireling approach" (John 10) by attempting to sell and peddle salvation and redemption when it should be free. Hmph. Do you know what's a trip about all of this? At the end of the day, it's all tied to spiritual narcissism.

So, why is it so rampant and why are very few church folks actually doing anything about it? Oh, that's where one of my all-time favorite insights about Scripture comes in. Peep what Revelation 21:8

(NKJV) states: *"But the **cowardly**, unbelieving, abominable, murderers, sexually immoral, sorcerers, idolaters, and all liars shall have their part in the lake which burns with fire and brimstone, which is the second death."* Uh-huh. While so many folks like to talk about what the sexually immoral and murderers are doing/have done, peep the very first folks listed who will make it to the second death: THE COWARDS.

A coward is "a person who lacks courage in facing danger, difficulty, opposition, pain, etc.; a timid or easily intimidated person" — and you can look at the state of the American Church right now and see that while there is a ton of Jezebel-ing going on in the pulpit, there are also a lot of cowards in the pews. For some reason, while the Apostle Paul made it crystal clear that *"For what have I to do with judging those also who are outside? Do you not judge those who are inside? But those who are outside God judges. Therefore, put away from yourselves the evil person'."* (I Corinthians 5:12-13 — NKJV) Meanwhile, church folks are doing the exact opposite. All kinds of foolishness are transpiring on Sabbath and Sunday, all over the globe (and especially on this continent), yet cowards are saying nothing and so the Jezebels are having an absolute ball. It's counterproductive. It's contrary to how the Bible says that church should be. It's also dangerous.

So, why am I so comfortable addressing it? Even though I don't participate in the nonsense (because a part of what comes with being an adult is knowing how to make your own decisions and not just following along with what your family is doing), that doesn't mean that I don't have accountability — and some of my "accountability team" are church leaders. In fact, I remember when one of my favorites once said to me, "Shellie, it's clear that you are a prophet. Who are you a prophet to?" One of the first things that I thought about was the Old Testament prophet Nathan — you know, David's messenger (2 Samuel 12). I definitely think that he and I are related (if you know about how

Nathan got down and then you know me, you get the correlation, for sure! — LOL). However, what I said was, "I know who I come for on a regular basis and it's church leadership," to which my spiritual friend said, "Welp. There you go."

Do I respect the position of church leadership? I do. Do I think that means that they should be revered as if they are untouchable or can't be corrected? I mean, if you actually believe that, you are caught up in one of the worst forms of idolatry, whether you realize it or not. *No one is above correction.* And honestly, since James 3 says that teachers are to be held to a higher standard and I Timothy 3 basically says that church leaders should be above reproach, if anyone needs to be held accountable to the utmost (and not just by those who their ego tells them is "worthy"), it's them — from the pastors *and their wives* (because a lot of these wives are totally out of control, for real) on down. Y'all, until/unless that happens, church is going to continue to be a lot like children who are in a home with narcissistic parents.

I mean, have you ever read what that looks like? Narcissistic parents give conditional love. Narcissistic parents will gaslight the entire mess out of you until you honestly don't know what's up from down or left from right. Narcissistic parents will somehow remember all of the wrong that was done to them and none of the wrong that they did to you. Narcissistic parents will want you to invalidate the pain that they caused you in order for them to appear perfect. Narcissistic parents will want you to constantly agree with them; according to them, challenging them in any way, even once you are an adult, is a peak form of disrespect. Narcissistic parents will love bomb you in order to gain your trust and then give you the silent treatment when you displease them. Narcissistic parents really only praise, reward and celebrate those who fit into their own little box of expectations...and sometimes demands.

Hmph. Now transfer that over to a lot of these churches out here and tell me that you don't get that a ton of church members are acting *just like children* who were victims of narcissistic abuse from their parents — only, it's the leadership that's doing it. And because there's not enough discussion about narcissistic parents or narcissistic church leaders, folks think that what they are doing is being "loyal to their church" when really, it's more like they are living like they've got a spiritual form of Stockholm Syndrome going on...as a direct result, they don't know how to let go.

And *that* circles back to why I haven't been a member of a church for years — because I grew up around so much narcissistic behavior, it had become normal to me. And so, I would tolerate the abuse. Basically, I grew up in a denomination that didn't protect me. Hmph. It's kind of wild because even the last Adventist pastor to rebaptize me (some of y'all could stand to research what mikvehs are and the purpose that they serve; Christians didn't come up with the concept of baptism — not by a long shot) gossiped worse than women and the last Adventist church that I attended regularly, that pastor is out here being a colossal fame chaser. My personal experience is that denomination has just been unsafe and unaccountable for so many years, on so many levels. At the same time, I visited churches where the egos, the nepotism (which is also a somewhat subtle form of narcissism) and the all-out hypocritical boldness was beyond rampant (I once had a pastor's wife come up to me and say, "You know that prostitutes in the Old Testament used to wear short hair like yours?" to which I replied, "OK, but you have on a wig." Uh-huh, and we ain't be right since. *Lawd, what made her think that she could come at me like that?* Her unchecked ego. Plain and simple.). In a healed state, I don't do unsafe anymore. I don't care if it's a friend, a family member or folks who are within church walls. And it's not that I don't support church, either. I just rally for the biblical version, not this mess that the West has come up with — the mess that is getting more carnal and unaccountable by the day.

As I was having (some of) this conversation with someone who complains, constantly, about the church that they attend here in Nashville and they said that I was a renegade, the first thing that came to my mind was the hip-hop song (the real ones know) that has the hook that says, "Renegade. Never been afraid to say what's on my mind any time of day…" and that would be accurate. The second was a verbally expressed: "Thank you." I know that a renegade is seen as an apostate, and honestly, I'm OK with that. Some folks need to remember that the Pharisees — CHURCH FOLKS — plotted to kill Christ himself because he wouldn't sit down, shut up and follow their traditional routine of nonsense (Matthew 12:14). Y'all, it really is time to stop saying that "the Church is a hospital" (when, in many ways, it's like a hospice), if folks are not going to actually get better…*for the better*. And for me, I got better — so much better — once I removed myself from spiritually narcissistic environments.

And that's why one of my main life mottos is "watch the tree" — and yes, that is a biblical reference. If a tree is indeed known by its fruit (Matthew 12:33), the Fruit of the Spirit includes the traits of "love, joy, peace, longsuffering, kindness, goodness, faithfulness, gentleness, self-control" (Galatians 5:22), and I have grown, exponentially so, in these areas since leaving spiritually narcissistic environments, *what is the problem?* There isn't one. Narcissists won't get that, though. They have to heal, on a billion different levels, in order to do so.

There's more ground to cover, so it's time to move on from this. I'll just end it with these points: One, you can't be a lover of Scripture and hate the Church that Scripture speaks of; however, you are deceiving yourself if you think that you should tolerate a narcissistic church environment. Two, do I hate Adventism? I wouldn't have chosen it, that's for sure. At the same time, I probably wouldn't be in the heightened Hebrew culture awareness that I'm in now without it and so, for that, I am grateful. Also, I do believe that every denomination has its strengths, and although a lot of Adventists seem to be obsessed with the last days (one of my favorite quotes is, "The excess of a virtue is a vice." Aristotle is credited for saying it), their breakdowns of Daniel and Revelation are top-tier. That said, I once read that one definition of hate is unwilling (which helped me to understand how a God of love can hate divorce — more on that later) and I am totally unwilling to stagnate my growth by returning to that space. And three, do I see myself returning to church again? Eh. I don't see myself returning to the churches that I once supported, at all — not as a member or regular by any means.

As a wise person once said, "When you know better, you do better." When I come into contact with a church that resembles Acts 2, that follows Christ in the sense of going on the Sabbath like he went into the temple on the true Sabbath day, I'm open.

Until then, I'll pray that Adventists learn that the Fourth Commandment isn't the only one (there are 10 — Exodus 20), that first-day folks truly learn to follow the customs of Yehoshua the Christ (including honoring the Sabbath) and that all of the spiritual narcissists up in these buildings will learn to humble themselves: *"For whoever exalts himself will be humbled, and he who humbles himself will be exalted."* (Luke 14:11 — NKJV)

Folks are unsafe in their presence until and unless they do.

They are a danger to themselves as well.

Hey, that's how narcissism works — yep, even within the Church. #Elmoshrug

"Family does not mean: keeping secrets;
walking on eggshells; lying about who
I am to keep the peace; pretending others are healthy
when they are not; tiptoeing around the truth;
attending holidays that derail my healing process;
defending poor choices; engaging in toxic behavior;
remaining loyal to old behaviors that no longer align
with my growth or assuming caretaking
responsibilities that are not mine to carry."

(UNKNOWN)

Chapter Three
Family. LAWD...FAMILY.

I'm a Black woman. I don't just mean that I was born Black or look Black. I mean that I am unapologetically pro-Black. I am very intentional about doing things that reflect that — and that requires delving into things about Blackness that sometimes, what I call "lowercase blacks" (because not all skin folk are kinfolk and that's just the truth), like to ignore or avoid as much as possible.

Take this thing called "family". Definitely one of the best things that ever happened to me is reading a book entitled, *Safe People: How to Find Relationships That Are Good for You and Avoid Those That Aren't* (Cloud/Townsend). Before checking it out, I didn't realize how much I needed to apply "safe" into my life — a big part of the reason is because it's not a word that I was very accustomed to.

Safe means things like "secure from liability to harm, injury, danger, or risk", "involving little or no risk of mishap, error, etc." and "dependable or trustworthy". Synonyms for safe include words like cherished, free from danger, protected, sheltered, shielded, uninjured, unmolested, preserved, unthreatened and vindicated. And let me tell you something: when it comes to my family? "Safe" is not even in the top 10 of words that I would use to describe my experience with being in one — I'm not just talking about my immediate family either. I mean, generationally so.

However, before I get deeper into my own bloodline, some general groundwork.

First, damn near everyone has some sort of dysfunction in their family dynamic — you know, "a malfunctioning part or element". Sadly, folks are so used to being in dysfunction with their DNA that I don't even think a lot of individuals get *just how dysfunctional* their household actually is — or was while growing up. If you're curious, some very telling signs of a dysfunctional family include: having members who don't take accountability for the hurt or harm that they cause (including trying to downplay what they've done or attempting to put more pressure on you to excuse their behavior or make them feel better about the damage that inflicted); having members who use intimidation to control others (or appearances); members who neglect, ignore or devalue the needs of certain family members based on "rank" (which is also a sign of narcissism); family members who tell other family members that their memories or feelings about them are wrong (usually to cover up the damage that they've done); family members who make victims "the bad guy" for the abuse that they endured (especially if they tell others about it); family members who suck at clear and direct communication; family members who respond quicker to emotions like sadness and fear than happiness and satisfaction (because they like being the "fix-it person" which is also typically tied to narcissism), and family members who have poor boundaries and/or don't respect the boundaries of children. If you're already triggered, chances are, you grew up in a really dysfunctional family environment.

OK, so let me expound, just a bit, on that boundaries thing. At the end of the day, boundaries are limits and even from birth, boundaries for children should be taught and developed. In fact, I think one of the easiest ways to define abuse is "violating someone's boundaries" — whether that be physical, mental, emotional, financial (you folks who like to use your children's social security numbers, etc. to get things, you are a financially abusive parent), spiritually or otherwise. And what's a good example of being spiritually abusive? I'll actually give you two: hiding behind Scripture, all the while acting like it's a "trump card" that should silence folks when you are called out on your own mess. Another is manipulating Scripture. A stellar example are parents — including parents of grown children — who think that they can railroad over their kids (especially their adult ones) by quoting "Honor your father and mother" (Exodus 20:12) as if the Good Book doesn't always say, "Do not provoke your children to wrath" (Ephesians 6:4). Yeah, some of y'all want to be highly prized and obeyed (umm, adult children do not have to obey you anymore, by the way) and yet, you conveniently choose to overlook the fact that YOU are to "avoid behaviors that can irritate or arouse feelings of anger, hurt, shame or fear"; there's no expiration date on that, by the way. If you want to use the Bible to get your children to do what you want them to do, stop being a hypocrite by not taking the instructions directed at you to heart as well.

One more thing. One of my all-time favorite quotes is "Adulthood is surviving childhood." What that basically means is there were a lot of us who grew up in a such a dysfunctional family environment, that much of our lives are spent unlearning toxicity, figuring out our own voice and understanding what should and should not be tolerated from our bloodline, so that we can, in turn, have healthy relationships with other people. I am definitely one of those individuals. And again, I'm not just speaking of the people who were in my home — as I'm typing this, I'm struggling to find where there wasn't textbook dysfunction going on...kinds that I oftentimes had a very front seat to.

That's not to say that there aren't things that, whenever I think about pretty much every relative that I have (or had because several have passed on), they didn't have their good points. My DNA, on both sides, is very smart, pretty ambitious and many of them have a solid sense of humor. Minus my paternal and maternal grandparents (my maternal grandmother doesn't really count because she died at age 53), I have at least a handful of good memories; unfortunately, my grandparents were just so arrogant and image-conscious that no bond was ever really solidified with them. Interestingly enough, I did have good relationships with *their* parents — well, my maternal grandmother's mother turned out to be a bit of a trip but...even with her, I can smile on some things, though.

As far as my aunts and uncles go, on my dad's side, it was a mixed bag. The ones who always knew that I was their niece, all but one of them were cool; the ones who found out, they were fine with me in concept, yet I had to do most of the work to maintain the relationships, and so, one day I just stopped. I haven't heard from them since, which confirmed my thoughts on the fact that I was the one who had to initiate the work all along: me, the younger one, the niece. In fact, when my father, their brother, died, even though their father was the one to tell me (more on that in an upcoming chapter, for sure), I never heard from any of them. Not one. Family, chile. On my mother's side, she only had a brother. He battled with substance abuse all of his life

— or hell, at least all of mine. I know he loved me, as best as someone with his battles could. When he died, I tried to cultivate a relationship with his own twin children; however, they were so broken and damaged from having drug-addicted parents that they were hustlers more than cousins, and so I had to put firm boundaries in place. Those boundaries remain to this day. Again, family, chile.

My immediate family? My dad is gone. When we get into the Libras in my life in another chapter, I'll tackle that more in-depth too. My brother? He's technically my half-brother, although I love him like he's my whole one. At the same time, because my mother and his father really complicated our lives, our relationship has layers, nuances and complexities. I do adore my brother in many ways; always will. He's the only sibling that I have. And what about my mother? Hmph. *My mother.*

Back when I wrote my first book, I was careful to not really get too much into our dynamic — a big part of it was due to fear not because I didn't have plenty to say — and remember, being fearful of a parent or having a parent who uses intimidation tactics, that ties into deep levels of toxicity and dysfunction. And as far as she goes, two tactics that she's damn near an Olympian at are the silent treatment and being passive-aggressive. In fact, when I let her know that I got my first book deal and then I told her what I would be writing about, she didn't speak to me for six whole months; I know it's because she thought that I was going to, let's go with "shed light", on so much of our stuff. These days, I'm not afraid of her, not in the least. I will say that the mercy that I spoke of in the foreword, she's getting a huge dose of it, because I am going to leave a lot of my trauma details out — both now and in the chapter that addresses us with more detail.

For now, I'll just say that pretty much all of my life, my boundaries have been disrespected—mentally, emotionally, physically, spiritually, relationally...you name it. In fact, I think a part of the reason why I allowed so much foolishness in my friendships and relationships is directly because of that. Because of what I grew up around, I thought that love meant having no boundaries and so I loved others just that way. Whew, is that toxic. I mean, what's a bigger word than toxic, actually? I'm definitely going to dive a bit more into this when I touch on how many of my past female friendships were unpredictable manifestations of my dynamic with my mother. Yes, straight up, adulthood is surviving childhood.

So, with that as-briefly-as-I-could-possibly-make-it breakdown, do I have a healthy relationship with any of my family? It's weird because I never really had blood family who took initiative other than my father (and he was so frustrated with my mother and his own family that he could've done a much better job) and a late second cousin who, in many ways, was a very selfish individual. If anything, I would go with the word "comical" to describe a lot of my interaction with my family — comical in a low-key pathetic kind of way. For instance, when my father died, his mother (a woman who rewrote history in his funeral program to make herself look good...again, narcissism) actually reached out, not to see if I was OK about losing my dad but to basically tell me that I should take custody of my favorite late uncle's (a child of hers who overdosed years prior to my dad's death) children. When I literally said to her, "Umm, I lost my dad. Thanks for asking how I am", she just started doing what she usually does: complaining about life. Or her ex-husband, my paternal grandfather — a man who mostly let his now late-wife run things as far as he and I were concerned (which is cowardly behavior and ultimately caused me to leave him all the way alone; more on that up the pike too), when his son basically "outed him" as my grandfather, I would get a $50 check in the mail and one time he gave me $1,200 toward a car. When I would go to see his family (who lives two hours away from me), not a picture of me (or my father) was in sight. I even remember staying at his friend's house who once said to me (in my 20s, mind you), "My best friend's last name is Warren. I wonder if the two of you are related." Absolutely amazing.

It's like, my extended family accepted that I existed yet sucked at proactively nurturing a genuine relationship. It was weird. And so, I think instead of the word "healthy", I'll just say that I learned to accept that, because there is also a lot of narcissism in my bloodline (because, interestingly enough, a lot of them are Adventists and I already broke that down), I learned to accept that they tended to care more about how things look/looked than how they actually were.

As a result, I ended up with quite a bit of what I call "love family" instead of "blood family". The best way to explain who those folks are, especially in Southern culture is, it's pretty common for parents to require that you call their close friends "aunt" or "uncle" — and yes, there were many people in my space who I was told to address in that manner. Looking back, if I had had children, I wouldn't have done that. Your friends don't make them mine. I need to respect them as your friends; however, I shouldn't be forced to embrace them as my own family. Honestly, all that does is confuse children when it comes to boundaries because you start expecting people to treat you like the title you gave them when it's a toss-up if that is going to be the case or not. Plus, as an ex-boyfriend of mine once said, "People tend to be the most loyal to the person they met first, no matter what."

Chile, I should Cash App him for that because the amount of people who were so either emotionally attached to or starstruck by the very people who hurt me to the point where they would justify, defend and make excuses for them — y'all ain't no family if you're trying to rationalize mistreatment. Y'all are actually a low-key accomplice and unsafe as literal hell (and again, in the wise words of Thomas Hobbes, "Hell is truth seen too late."). Again, *family should be safe*. FAMILY SHOULD BE A SAFE SPACE — the family you didn't choose (blood) and the family that you did choose (love).

And just what does my family interaction look like now, especially since I am the type of person who takes the quote "adulthood is surviving childhood" very literally and seriously? Blood relatives, I'm pretty good on (if you know slang jargon, you can pretty much read between the lines on that). Folks who married into the family? Let me just put it to you this way: Have y'all ever noticed that stepparenting is not a biblical concept? And before some of you start, no, Joseph was not Christ's "stepfather"; he was his *earthly* dad. Christ had a very real and functional relationship with his Father and Mary was never Adonai's wife. Yeah, I find it to be extremely disrespectful, every time I hear that someone try and rationalize not honoring marital covenant (because Matthew 19:1-12 and I Corinthians 7:10-11 are very clear about what adultery actually is and how divorced folks are supposed to move) by saying that. The actual truth and reality are that Scripture took marriage far too seriously for people to come into broken covenants and then just assume the role of the original parent. So that has never sat well with me in my family — a family that comes from a long line of divorces and multiple spouses. You can (for example) be my mother's husband; you are not a "second father", though. Not by any stretch. Let's not live lies. And love family — the people who my parents picked, I've phased out of a lot of them because of what I already said about the whole loyalty thing. If I've shared my pain and you're constantly on some, "I mean, it couldn't have been all of that" or "Are you sure you're not exaggerating?" then we really don't have much to talk about. All you're doing is revictimizing me so...go... be over there. And then there are some who, when I stopped calling, we stopped talking. I spent a lot of years being codependent; it's such a counterproductive waste of time. When people value you, they will prioritize you; when they prioritize you, they will make time for you. The concept isn't complicated. I now have love family whom I chose and I feel cherished, nourished and extremely safe around them. Daily, I give thanks.

Sometimes, when I am in an interview, the topic of family comes up and I'm asked if I feel lonely that I am not particularly close to anyone at this stage and season of my life — and you know what, I don't have to pause and reflect or tiptoe around the answer. My response is always an immediate, "No. Not really." I think it has a lot to do with some of the things that my father and I discussed, deeply, in the months leading up to his death. He wanted — and deserved — love and acceptance so badly from his own family (both sides, too, because he's a survivor of a TON of abuse, neglect and abandonment) that it resulted in him using drugs and alcohol to cope with the excruciating pain. Oh, how we've done folks such a colossal disservice by causing them to think that they should stick around toxic family relational dynamics because it's "the right thing to do". *I mean, who even came up with that?* My guess is, it was a toxic family member who was trying to take advantage of another family member at the time and so that BS came out of their mouth.

Me? I am a generational curse-breaker; therefore, words cannot express how committed I am to not repeat my father's ending. Even though I used to have suicidal ideations (in part due to the my own abusive experiences and also because I honestly believe that level of internalized stress manifests itself on both sides of my family tree), there is no way that I'm going to let my father's only child and end of his legacy (because I'm not going to have any kids, so after me, when it comes to him, it's a wrap) repeat his patterns — and that means that extreme measures must be taken...and they have been.

And you know what? The more space that I've had away from the people I didn't choose — both blood and love — the more time that I've had with those who I did (love-wise) and the more that I am able to heal because of that...the things that I have gotten from my family — my maternal grandmother's hands; the women on my father's side's full breasts; both of my great-grandmother's unique take on style; my paternal grandfather's interest in knowledge; most of my uncles' wild senses of humor; my father's love for all things music; my mother's interest in all things Scripture; both of my parents ambivert traits along with half of my face that is my mom's and half of my face that is my dad's along with a skin tone that is a blend of the both of them — I can celebrate those things within me because I get that, literally, for better or for worse, I wouldn't exist without those individuals. At the same time, though, each generation should supersede the other, and if that means going totally against "how it's always been done" because how it's always been done has been dysfunctional, so be it.

...

You know, it's interesting because, a former spiritual mentor of mine, when he once asked me what I wanted most out of life and I simply said, "I just want to be healthy", I'll never forget what his reply was: "Good luck with that. The healthier you get, the lonelier you'll be."

I mean, yes — and no. My ambivert nature actually likes to take the "less is more" approach as far as human interaction goes and so I wouldn't say that I'm lonely. I have a tight tribe, I coach quite a few people and I really like myself, so I don't mind spending time alone. I do get his ultimate point, though: When you are willing to pay the high price that comes with being a whole, sound and sane individual, you find yourself realizing just how rare it is to really walk that road. Indeed, our culture celebrates brokenness and dysfunction; hell, it basically normalizes it.

And as far as being good with not "playing the game" in order just to have family members around, for the cynics who are probably thinking, "You say that now. Girl, you go through something for real and then report back" — I did. On December 22, 2021, my HVAC blew up my townhouse...and yes, I mean that it literally did just that. And although the fire marshal didn't exactly say that, had I been home at the time, I would've died, what he did say was, unless I was on the bottom steps and facing the front door when the explosion happened, "It wouldn't have gone well for you at all." And just where was I when it all went down? I was getting waxed and buying some new bras. In fact, after I saw the fire and confirmed the cause, I even kept the pedicure appointment that I had for later that day. Talk about a peace that passes all understanding, chile.

Anyway, the way that I handled that entire day — shoot, season — of my life, it let me know that some things in me had shifted, drastically so too. For one thing, I didn't call one relative about it (to this day, I still haven't). I called the people who I chose to be in my life: the ones who I could trust, the ones who wouldn't incite fear or paranoia, the ones who I knew would have my back...fully. *And they did.*

I also peeped the level of calm that I had — one that I know would've been a struggle for me had I kept certain folks from my bloodline in my life because they always seem to lean into the negative. Without their influence and energy, I was unruffled when it came to losing my place (and 90 percent of the items in it), losing one of my main paying gigs a month later and trying to figure out what life was trying to teach me throughout most of 2022. Throughout that entire time, my chosen love family never wavered, and, in some ways, offered some unexpected and supernatural support. Looking back, that season was difficult *and* confirming. I have no regrets...across the board. I am stronger, I am clearer, and I am healthier. Whatever I had to lose or remove — person, place, thing or idea — to get here, it was totally worth it. And then some.

You know, I once read a quote that said, "Let's get out of the habit of telling people 'That's still your mom, your dad or your sister.' You are allowed to walk away from people who constantly hurt you." Pass the plate, fifteen times on that.

Family can be a beautiful thing. You'll get no arguments from me there. Yet if it's at the expense of your holistic safety and peace of mind, it's time to do some serious shifting. A lot of people are out here suffering, unnecessarily so, because they are loyal to dysfunction — and yes, that is a super toxic way of thinking. And living.

Bottom line with this chapter is, if the blood family who you didn't choose isn't good for and to you, choose some love family who will be. It's as simple, and sometimes challenging, as that.

Believe me, I know.

"*Grief and love are conjoined; you don't get one without the other.*"

(JANDY NELSON)

Chapter Four

My Father and My Fiancé
Are Both Libras. They're Also
Both Gone Now.

Since I do coach couples and write about relationships, I'm pretty used to people asking me for advice. If it happens to be a Black man who wants to be with a Black woman (statistics say that the majority of Black men do, by the way — some of y'all need to stop believing everything that's on TikTok), one thing that I almost always advise is "Be with a Black male advocate." Why do I say that? Well, for one thing, Black men need the kind of women who study, research and aggressively seek to understand the challenges that come with being a Black man in this country. Secondly, it absolutely ties into something that an ex-boyfriend of mine once said; something that I totally agree with: "A woman should be a man's sanctuary." When that man is Black, being his "place of refuge", especially within the United States, is 10,000 percent what he needs. And although, yes, on a surface level, I believe that speaks to the type of wife that a woman should be, honestly, I think that *all women* should want to be a safe and peaceful space for men. That said, when it came to my father, he didn't really get that from most of the women in his life. His two grandmothers came the closest, for sure. Everyone else, though? Oh, how they failed. Miserably so. And the men in his life? In many ways, they were even worse.

Because of that, the way that I always described the relationship that I had with my father is that I know, without question, that he loved me; problem was, I also could tell that he didn't love himself very much — and, as "PTSD Shellie" has moved into "Real Shellie", I think that is the pattern of men that I oftentimes chose to involve myself with too. For instance, my first love has always reminded me a lot of my father: really smart, quick witted, very affirming…also, in situations of his own choosing, he complained quite a bit, was weak when it came to certain substances and many of his family dynamics were dysfunctional as hell. *Literally.* Toward me? He never (EVER) wavered in professing his love for me while also never fully providing what I needed due to the complexities of his own life. Like I said, he and my father reflected so much of one another (both were/are very handsome men as well).

As far as my dad goes, a good example of this is the fact that, when it came to my birthday, he never missed it. However, my graduations and special events that required going to DFW to come to BNA? Never once did that happen. Backstory: Since my parents divorced when I was three and the way that he found out that it was going down incensed him so (based on his version, he was blindsided, for sure), although he would always make a big deal about "my day" (and other special days) via cards with money in them and boxes with gifts in them, while he was living in both Lincoln, Nebraska (where I was born) or Dallas, Texas, never once did he come to see me. According to him, he loathed Huntsville, Alabama, where his father lived (due to their broken dynamic) and because of the particular Adventist college that is there and Nashville, Tennessee, due to how he felt about my mother — and so, I had to pay the price. Yeah, that's another thing that I found myself gravitating to: men who were absorbed so much in their own stuff that my own needs had to take the backseat...almost constantly.

Anyway, even though I only saw my father for a few weeks every summer while growing up, he did make sure to make those times as special and memorable as he could. He also was intentional about us speaking to each other on a weekly basis in between. Because of that, my memories of him include him serenading me regularly with Lou Rawls's song, "You'll Never Find"; him saying that the Prince classic, "When Doves Cry" reminded him exactly of his parents (and boy, did he play it often); him being able to play the entire hell out of the bass, piano and organ (his father even admitted to me once that he neglected nurturing my father's music ability; I'll keep the rest of what he said to myself because...mercy); him having really good style; him almost always having on a pair of sunglasses that had my initials in a corner of them; us taking professional pictures together every year; him purchasing me an ice-skating outfit and ice-skating being our "traditional date" until I became an older teen; Lord, that man calling me during damn near every Dallas Cowboys game on Sundays during football season (which makes football season semi-difficult for me now that he's gone); him rarely, ever, calling me "Shellie"—most of the time it was "Big Girl" or "You Ole' Fat Leg"; his vinyl record collection being one that could rival any record store (no exaggeration on that); him saying that while he was not fond of my mother (that's the clean version), he did think that I was pretty like her and that I had half of both of their faces (I have their wedding album and I would be inclined to agree; my mouth is him all day long—physically and literally because we're both hella candid and direct); us sharing a mutual love for random research and information (which took up a lot of our phone conversations and email exchanges); his love for stray cats, which was kind of excessive (the counselor in me feels like he was that way because of his own abandonment issues), and the way people naturally gravitated to his personality (especially when it came to his laugh, his musical ability and the way that he was gonna dance — wherever and whenever, chile). My father? He didn't make a lot of enemies — except when it came to himself. I understand why too.

Although, not once, did my father ever put his hands on me or call me out of my name (he was the safe parent in that way), he was a functional substance abuser — one that his grandmothers (who rarely called him his actual name, which we will get to in a minute; they referred to him as "Sarge") tried to hide from me. When you're a kid, you never wonder things like, "If I mainly came to Dallas to see my dad, why am I staying with you, Grandma Katie?" and when you're older, it takes a while for you to say things like, "Umm, why is it that every time I call, you say this man is in the bathroom?" Looking back, I get that my father lived across the street from or next door to my Grandma Katie because a lot of the time, he was drunk or high and I just didn't know it. And those "bathroom breaks"? They were oftentimes binges or times when he was in jail due to a drug charge (probably another reason why my first love's street life didn't really alarm me).

Anyway, my dad almost always held down jobs (hell, he worked for the state and would take me to work with him for years) and I never really saw him angry — I did see him hurt, though, A LOT — and so the reality of what was truly going on didn't really hit me. That is, until after becoming an adult and being able to recognize what a drunken stupor actually looked like, I found myself getting tired of him randomly calling me to complain about his mother or mine (or just women, in general) or ranting about how much he couldn't stand his father or a woman named Mrs. Anderson from back in Lincoln, or the abuse that he endured at the hand of some of his mother's husbands and a church leader once, or how (surprise, surprise), he was sick of the hypocrisy of Adventism and church folks, in general. And so, before long, because I knew that these were habits that he wasn't going to break, I started to ask questions. Lots and lots of questions.

Ugh. So much neglect, abandonment, abuse and secrets surrounded his birth — and his death. It's almost like the backstory of his name stood as the central theme of his life. And what is the backstory? Bottom line, until I was about 12 or 13, I thought that my father's first name was Eugene. His full name is actually Mervyn Eugene Warren. He revealed this to me by taking me to a parking lot once and showing me a neon sign that had "Mervyn" on it (it is a clothing store from back in the day). According to him (and my mother cosigned), his father asked him to change his name, so that the son that he had with another woman could be a "Jr." (amazing). I believe that his other son's middle name is "Edwin". My father decided to go by "Eugene". He never went by Mervyn, at least in my presence. When I confronted my grandfather about all of this in later years, it was fascinating. Chile, there are so many secrets and flat-out lies in my family tree, who knows? However, what I was told is that my grandparents were high school sweethearts, they did get married and yet, when they got pregnant with my dad, they attended separate colleges and so their parents (and grandparents) decided to raise my father. When my grandmother wanted a divorce, my grandfather moved on with another woman whose family told him that if he wanted to be a part of their family, he had to leave his son behind (gee, how Christlike). So, he paid child support yet didn't have a relationship with him. There must be some truth to this because I didn't know anything about those folks in Huntsville until I was a preteen — and it wasn't because my grandfather said a mumbling word. Actually, it was his son (the other Mervyn) who "outed" him once my mother decided to manage a group that he was in at the time. Hmm...she claimed that she didn't tell me all of this herself because she didn't want the "Huntsville Warrens" to reject me. OK, but you felt good about managing their son? Suddenly, their character can be trusted? Make it make sense, chile.

Anyway, interestingly enough, while I was penning this book and looking for a certain thing about my father, Google provided me with the official wedding announcement of my parents in the *Poughkeepsie Journal*, dated June 21, 1972. I actually turned that bad boy into a T-shirt — or a few reasons. One, it's a part of my history. Two, it's proof of my father having the name Mervyn. And three, it reminds me to continue to side-eye my mother about something she says as far as the origin story of her and my dad. Mercy abounds again, so I won't get into the details. She knows what I mean when I say that, though. Documented history will always trump the versions of stories that we tell ourselves because we don't want to face the reality of the actual truth and the roles that we play in it. Yeah, that's why I've always liked the Message Version of Ecclesiastes 7:18: *"It's best to stay in touch with both sides of an issue. A person who fears God deals responsibly with all of reality, not just a piece of it"* — and although there is no way that I can break down all of my father's life or our life together in one chapter, that is enough to give you a peek into our dynamic. I was loved, deeply so, by a very broken man. And as PTSD Shellie has transitioned into the Real Shellie, again, I get that how he treated cats without a home is oftentimes how I have loved equally broken men. Yes, fathers play a role in how daughters see men. It's DNA. It's also been proven.

OK, so let me tie in something real quick. Back when *Inside of Me* came out, it took my father a long time to even consider reading it. I gave him the brief synopsis of what it was about and he basically said, "Hell naw." It's not because he couldn't handle *my* vices; in fact, something that I always respected about my dad is the fact that he was so open about his own that he never made me feel any type of way about the things that I had done; that definitely wasn't the reality on my mother's side. Nah, he wanted to pass on the book because after I found out *the real truth* behind my parent's divorce (details spared because, again, mercy) and then he learned of all of the drama and trauma that I endured, in part, due to the fall out behind that truth, he said, "Unless you want some folks to die, I'm better off not reading it." Again, the candor. The directness. The "It is what it is" (even though I actually hate that phrase, it's fitting here). Those things about my personality, I definitely attribute to him.

So, since my parents divorced when I was three (interestingly enough, my mother also remarried a week before I turned four; do with that what you will), my father and I had a unique type of relationship. I already shared what a lot of it consisted of, including the "*Jeopardy*-like" tidbits that became the norm for our dialogue. In fact, while prepping to write this chapter, as I was combing through some emails to see what we discussed the most, aside from him commenting on almost every devotional that I would write (I penned those for about 18 years, pretty much three times a week), I noticed that we had our own theme because, something that my father would oftentimes say to me after I shared an insight was, "You are not human, girl."

Why would he say something like that? According to him, one reason had to do with his thoughts about my mother at the time of my conception (chile). Another is because he said that my connection with God was unlike any other that he had ever witnessed before. And so, since he knew that a lot of my book was filled with many of the struggles that he couldn't "save me" from, he'd rather not know about them; especially when it came to the sexual abuse that I had experienced — *especially* since it was at the hands of someone who he actually had encountered himself once upon a time; even then, that same man couldn't respect a boundary to save his life. Hmph. That seemed to be the norm for my dad: surrounded by people who broke boundaries to the point where he used drugs and alcohol to numb the pain of that reality.

Fast forward to the year leading up to his demise (which, from all of the information I gathered, was a suicide; I actually learned more about what happened to him from his landlord than anyone in my "family"), I knew something was off. As funny and fun as my dad tended to be, more times than not, he was also such an emotional self-cutter at times. Some years back, when I did some digging into why, although I don't respect a lot of what his father told me, what I *do* respect is that, when I asked him to give me his unedited truth about why he, quite frankly, sucked so much as a father to the only child of his four that actually looks like the spitting image of him, he was very real about it. He didn't deflect. He didn't pass the buck. He owned that in many ways, he was a coward at the time, because I don't know how you can marry into a family who wants you to not acknowledge your own flesh and blood — I don't care what the times were like. Again, spiritual narcissism is a mutha on so many levels and in so many ways.

And I guess that is why, months before I received the news that my dad had died, it made all of the sense in the world that the Holy Spirit would tell me to "release" that side of his family, along with my father's mother. There is not enough time or space to get into the millions of reasons why. What I will share is that the last year of my father's life, because we did have very deep, hard and graphic conversations — about his childhood, my parents' marriage, his life choices, his substance abuse, you name it — I think that I knew that I needed to emotionally prepare myself for the months that were to bring some "You *can't* be serious" moments. Yeah, I think that, subconsciously, I knew something life-altering was coming because I found myself saying to him, more than once, "Whatever you're about to do, can you wait until I at least turn 40?" It's another message for another time that something that I get from my mother (because again, DNA) is sensing when some people are about to transition out of this life. My dad died in March. I turned 40 that following June. The last email exchange that we had was February 28. We hadn't spoken on the phone for over a month prior to that.

How did I find out that he was gone? Welp, as life would have it, his father. I was on the phone with a friend and an email from him popped up asking me to give him a call. Nothing in me was moved...or scared. I almost blandly said to my friend, "Girl, either his mother or my father is dead. I already know" — because, somewhere deep within, I *did* already know. Again, when I was instructed to "release", I knew that it was in preparation for...*something*. Anyway, when I finally found the energy to call and my grandfather said, "The landlord found your father....", everything trailed off similar to how things sounded over the phone when I first heard the news about my late fiancé, back in

November of 1995. The only — well, main — difference this time was, unlike when I heard about Damien, when it came to my dad, I was very calm; almost eerily so.

Me: "So, what are you planning to do?"

Grandfather: "I wanted to hear your thoughts." (*Chile, no you didn't. Not really. When do you ever? You are gonna do what you wanted to do regardless. It's your way.*)

I knew my father. On many levels, very well. We both had even discussed our death and funerals before and so I simply said, "Have him cremated, spread his ashes over the Cowboys stadium, have a shot on him and go home. Oh, and whatever you do, I'm not coming."

Him after seeming surprised about saying that I didn't want to come to his send-off: "I'll just call his mother to see what she wants to do." Yep. That tracks. You've always been pretty dismissive, so why stop being that way now? Had that man ever even kissed me on the cheek or forehead before? I don't have one memory of it.

Anyway, my response to him wasn't flippant. It was quite calculated. The man, my father, who had an uncanny athletic gift and yet was denied by his family to see what it could become because most of the school games were on the Sabbath had gotten to the point where, once his body had aged significantly due to all of the damage that substance abuse had done, he got a job parking cars at the Cowboys stadium to watch what he couldn't do; the man who, because his musical abilities weren't nurtured like his siblings' were, he ultimately ended up playing in bars for shots; the man who told me out of his own mouth that the last thing he wanted was people who "couldn't be bothered" to see him while he was alive, standing over and gawking at him once he was dead — when I told his father, my grandfather, how to at least honor his firstborn, the only child who looks just like him, in death...he went ahead and did what *looked* right instead of what *was* right.

And why did I decide not to go? Oh, I told him why: "I don't have the energy to make people who played a role in how my father ended up feel better. I'll be at home. Please do tell me what you decide to do, though." After that, we pretty much hung up. Yep, my father and I had already discussed what I would do when his time came as well. I had no desire to photo-op deception. I had no desire to grin with people who played a starring role in so much of his pain. I had no desire to act like things were good or right when they weren't. I would grieve around those who I could trust. In fact, I don't recall any family being fully present in my loss. When I told my mother, after she said, "He did love you, Shellie", she called back the next day to say, "[My husband] had to hold me because I lost someone too." Umm, you haven't spoken to my father in 25 years and you both said, ever since I can remember, that you were not fans of each other and somehow, *this became about you?* Amazing. Then add tax. Narcissism abounds.

Fast forward, 6-8 weeks later, and not a word as far as an update goes. I didn't know when or how my father was funeralized, where he was buried — even really and truly what happened to him. Oh, but I was still receiving close-to-obnoxious forwards ("obnoxious" because why are you sending me emails from the college where your husband works and my father and I aren't really fans of? I absolutely do not care) from my grandfather's wife. I really wanted to send a nothing but cuss-laden reply; however, I simply said, "Please unsubscribe." From there, it turned into a full day's worth of email exchanges where I'm asking why she is discussing my dad with me at all and her saying things like, "We never told you what happened because we figured that you didn't want to be bothered." (That is a literal quote, by the way.) Umm, you thought that I didn't want to know what my dad died from or where his final resting place is, yet you *did* think I'd give a damn about what's happening at a college in Huntsville? *You really want that other side of me to come out, don't you?* The irony never escaped me that the bloodline who said that my dad should be denounced in life is the same bloodline that was gaslighting his only child in his death. Had I not emotionally released these people prior to his shift, there's no telling how ugly things could've gotten. I had already been warned that things would be strange; I had taken that warning very seriously.

After saying to her, more than once, that her husband should be the one having this conversation with me, *not her* (he never got in on the exchange, by the way), I finally got sick of it all and said, "This is what you've wanted all along, anyway. Consider me dead along with my father since things were always so difficult for you." A few weeks later, I received a funeral program and a typed sentence about what I was looking at from my grandfather. It appeared to be a typical funeral, with my grandfather and two of my dad's remaining brothers present, along with some of his AA buddies (seeing the AA friends was nice, I must say; my dad did speak fondly of some of them). As I read the program, I knew I made the right decision not to attend, because his mom took the time to literally rewrite history. I knew plenty about her relationship with my father and it wasn't as warm, fuzzy and functional as she tried to make it be. I did find it fascinating that, apparently, she didn't attend either. Hmph. DNA is a funny thing. She once told me that we both had four abortions in common. Not going to her firstborn's and me not going to my dad's funeral? Now we had that in common too (apparently, not attending funerals of relatives is in my DNA also...due to dysfunction...shocking, right?).

Beyond that, I knew nothing. I actually had to track down my dad's former landlord to get some sort of details. What he told me was that in the weeks leading up to my dad's death, he "fell off of the wagon" and was drunk a lot. Since my father had lived at the same address for 11-12 years (from what I did hear, his father would help with the rent sometimes) and would go in to say "hello" to management often, the landlord learned his patterns. He said that he had wrecked his car, fell down a flight of stairs and did some other self-destructive things in the weeks leading up to his death. However, it was when he didn't come into the office to say "hi" for a few days that he did a wellness check and found him dead in his apartment. From the way he said that my dad was positioned, it sounded similar to how my favorite uncle, his half-brother, was found years before.

A part of me will always wonder if that was a calculated move on my father's part. He felt so unheard by his parents in many ways, maybe he was going out loudly in his death. The landlord also said that some people came and ransacked my dad's place for some paperwork (hmm...wonder who that was and what they were looking for) and then said that the rest of this things could be trashed. For a few months after that, I kept trying to get the landlord to send me a few things: my bronzed baby shoes and Cowboy football helmet that he had gotten me as a child along with his vinyl collection. Initially, he agreed and yet, when I couldn't get in touch with the guy anymore, I resigned myself to the fact that other than pictures that I always had of me and my father, I now had basically nothing. And so, in honor of him, I actually purchased a Dallas Cowboys football jersey with his name on it (I need to get another one because it got lost in my house fire). That's pretty much the story. Over and out.

...

People will sometimes ask me what it was like to lose my dad at 39. I dunno — I actually continue to be more baffled that I lost a fiancé at twenty-one. What's wild is the fact that it wasn't until my dad died that I realized they had something in common: both of them were Libras. And then I realized that a lot of my favorite people (especially men) also were born under that same sign (Libras are known for being charming, intelligent and sociable). Nothing is random in life when you're really paying attention and so, I gave all of that some thought: What about my dad and Damien were similar? ANYTHING?

- They both had a love for music. Profoundly so.
- They both repped their city on a whole 'nother level. LOL.
- They both were spiritual beings yet not really religious.
- They both didn't make enemies with strangers.
- They both were quite charismatic.
- They both were very calculated in who they allowed to get close to them.
- They both were extremely observant.
- They both had one hell of a sneaky side.
- They both loved me very deeply.
- They both died too young.

And I got to experience them both — I saw what it's like to be loved by a wounded man and then what it was like to be loved by a man who came from married parents who invested in him his entire life and made sure that his needs were met; a man who wasn't abused or a substance abuser...a man who loved from a healed place.

Something else that my dad and Damien had in common is they both thought that I was a super rare find — both the wounded and healed man could see that. And now, almost 30 years into Damien's death and 10 into my father's (both anniversaries are in 2025), at the brink of 50, I see them both...clearer than I ever have.

So, to the two men who loved me, probably more than any of the others — I love you, I miss you, I see you too. Like a prism, there are so many sides that continue to reflect — even now.

Daddy, your legacy ends with me. I will go out strong. Promise you that.

Damien, romantically, you loved me better than any other man, to this day — still. Your death will not be in vain. I will not settle.

Two Libras — so different and yet, had me in common. AMAZING. Thank you.

"I knew I wasn't dealing with a person;
I was dealing with concepts, and once I investigated
the concepts about my mother, I had unraveled
all my concepts about everyone and everything."
(BYRON KATIE)

Chapter Five

So, Here's What My Mother and Past Female Relationships Have in Common

I've got to be honest and say that if there's one chapter that I kept putting off, it's this one. It's not because I don't have plenty to say (believe you me) — it's more due to what I mentioned in the beginning of this offering: I need to extend some mercy...and, to tell you the truth, there is one person in my life where that is very difficult for me to do. It's not because I haven't forgiven her for so much of what she's done (if you don't believe me, read her own book, where she writes about how much I've forgiven although she was extremely vague about what those things actually were) — it's more like, the levels of dysfunction and boundary-breaking have so many nuances to them and so much consistency in them that I've been trying to figure out how to be gracious in my approach.

Welp. Here goes nothin', chile.

To say that mothers and daughters have a complex relationship is like the understatement of the year; especially once you become an adult. My mother and me, though? Complex is a very polite word. I think what would actually be more accurate is "intense". You don't have the time and I don't have the space to get into all of the reasons and ways that have brought me to this conclusion. At the same time, I do think that my last physical interaction with her — one that was a few years ago at this point — sums it up pretty well. Well, actually, I think that I should talk about the last two in order to provide some context.

My friends oftentimes tease me that I act like I'm in my own self-induced witness protection program. They say that because only one person currently knows where I live (and that's just for safety's sake), only two other people have my mailing address (and they are out of state) and I can literally count how many people have my phone number. Some of this is because I am an ambivert (look that word up sometime). Another reason is because, since I spend a lot of time helping people for a living, I simply don't want a ton of folks having constant access to me. And still, another reason is because I have a mother who couldn't care less about boundaries. Not mine anyway. She never really has. I doubt she ever will. And that has given me some serious PTSD that I will probably be working through, on some level, for the rest of my life.

That's because, when your boundaries are treated like they are totally irrelevant, that sets up the perfect storm for abuse — "abnormal use" as Dr. Phil puts it (it's one of the few things that he says that I actually jive with) — of all sorts of things and in all sorts of ways...and yes, that makes me a survivor of abuse on a myriad of different levels. Although some people who I consider to be my tribe know the depths of what I mean, again, to be merciful, I'll leave a lot of the details out. Let's just say that the fact that I believe in God at all when so many of my family members, who claim to be Christians, were showing all the way out in the privacy of their own homes...some of them, my homes too? It even blows *my* own mind to ponder and reflect. I think I'll also put on record that my mom came from a home that consisted of an alcoholic father who was quite the spiritual hypocrite (pretty much until he died) and a super toxic marriage — and again, people tend to do what's familiar more than what's right. Drinking? I don't know if I've ever seen her do that. Toxicity, though? Again, you don't have the time and I don't have the space...or even all of the energy. I'll just say that she really needs to be thankful rather than resentful about how I am approaching this chapter. If I was trying to be vindictive, I would be saying a helluva lot more. After she reads this, unless she is just choosing to go into full denial mode, she will absolutely know that I have been kind.

Let me also say this: No, not every day — or sometimes even every week — in my house was some type of hell (again, according to Thomas Hobbes, "Hell is truth seen too late."). I will say that it was very unpredictable in there, though, mostly because how my mother emotionally processes things made growing up very stressful; far too stressful for a child or teenager to have to endure. On the upswing, I should also share the fact that I recognize that certain things about how I prioritize spirituality and how domesticated I naturally am (especially on the cooking tip) came from her. So does my unique take on fashion (our tastes are nothing alike, yet she is a New Yorker and definitely raised me to "buck Nashville" and cultivate a style of my own) and how I adore so many things about creativity. My love for reading, movies and my interest in pop culture, that definitely comes from her influence. And there are definitely days when she looks back at me in the mirror whether it's due to features of hers that I share or facial expressions of hers that I just can't seem to shake.

Yeah, my mother is my mother. I'm not mad about that. Also, I don't think that she's a monster. We are estranged, though. And it was my choice. And I don't regret it. Oh, and while we're here, although this book isn't about the PTSD of my people who are descendants of slaves, I do think that it should also go on record that it's mighty fascinating how triggered folks tend to get whenever they hear that someone no longer has a relationship with a family member. Hmph. The same folks who will tell you that you are insane (remember that the definition of insanity is doing the same thing while expecting a different result) for keeping a relationship going with someone who is mistreating you if they *aren't* your blood, they will then try and guilt the complete and entire hell out of you for removing yourself from DNA who does the same thing, especially in Black culture. Listen, whenever someone tries to challenge me on that, all I hear in my head is, "I mean, yo' mama can't be as bad as massa...". Goodness people, do you want folks to avoid hurt and harm — or not? Where do all of the bizarre caveats come from?

Besides, if anyone should be synonymous with feeling safe, it's family. Safe means things like "secure from liability to harm, injury, danger, or risk" and "dependable or trustworthy". If they are unsafe, it is my personal opinion (by the way, there are plenty of mental health experts who will back me here) that *you are insane* to stick around just because you share blood ties with them. Sometimes "honoring your parents" means accepting that they choose to not change, and so you need to leave them alone, so that you can do the growing, healing and transforming that you long to do because any parent worth anything would want their seed to supersede them — and sometimes that requires no longer being involved with them in order for that to actually transpire.

That said, when I first made my decision in my 40s to fully release my mother from my life, several people tried to challenge me on all of this (by the way, it's actually becoming more and more popular for adult kids to no longer have relationships with their parents because people are learning to take their mental and emotional health more seriously). However, after watching how my healing process has been going, many of those very same individuals have now said, "You are definitely way calmer without her in your life." *Gee, ya think?* When you're not being controlled by someone, when you're no longer operating from a place of fear of someone, you'd be amazed how much that can remove anxiety from your world.

One more thing before providing examples that caused me to make the decision that I did to be estranged: I think I also should share that even when you are someone who coaches or counsels for a living, you still need your own professional to go to. That said, whenever I speak to my, what I call "therapist friend", sometimes when we talk about what growing up with my mom was like, even *she* can't keep from having a look of shock when I tell her about some of the stuff that I survived when it comes to my relationship with my mother — not just as a child, adolescent or even young adult; hell, even well past that, life was semi-wild. As I self-reflect, now more than ever, I definitely think all of this is a part of the reason why I decided to "hard pass" on becoming a mother myself (interestingly enough, one time my mother said, out of the blue, to me, "I'm sorry for the role that I played in your abortions"). To be honest, very few women in my family, on either side of the tree, impress me when it comes to that particular role. While most of them turned out to be professionally extraordinary, in the maternal lane — eh, not so much. Personally, I think that some didn't really want to be moms. Others did it because it was expected of them. And some, they just didn't know how to be healthy mothers because it wasn't modeled to them, and, unfortunately, they didn't know how to admit that to themselves and others. Sad. Very sad.

OK, so far as all of the particulars that brought me to the point and place of no longer having a relationship with my mother, I think I've said enough. I'm on the brink of 50 and she's in her 70s. For the most part, she should "beat me to the punch", her eulogy will be pretty impressive, and I don't want to mar that; she's earned the praise and accolades that she will receive, no question. I think saying that it simply is unhealthy for me to try and deal with someone who refuses to take my boundaries seriously, year after year, is enough — at least for now...as far as details go. I do think that the final straws are important to let you in on, though, mostly because I know that someone reading this is currently trying to figure out what they should do about a bloodline family member breaker in their own universe.

OK, so back to the instances that I've been kinda dancing around. Indeed, my mom has never really been the person to take "no" for an answer. I think that's part of what will cause her to receive a national level of media attention whenever it's time for her to leave this earth; ironically, it's also a huge part of why I choose to be estranged from her. She's always had a way of politely telling you what you're going to do and if you're going to like it, usually in a very soft-spoken-initial-ly-nonthreatening-yet-very-cryptically-forceful kind of way. And what if you refuse? She'll just find a way to make you do it anyway. This is how I remember her being, especially when it comes to me, damn near all of my life. It could even be something that I want to wear that she doesn't like (when I was in my 20s) or trying to force me to stay with her at someone's home who she is visiting (when I was in my 30s).

And maybe that's why, 8 times out of 10, when I knew that she was coming from overseas to visit, I would close to hyperventilate (my tribe can certainly vouch for that); it's because I knew that she would be moving some of my furniture, and/or attempting to put me on a curfew in my own house, and/or having people come over to my place without asking me first, and/or wanting to run my electronic devices however she saw fit, and/or making passive-aggressive statements about how I chose to live my life, and/or not really respecting my own schedule if it contradicted with whatever her plans were, and/or asking me questions that were absolutely none of her business because I am an adult (like who I've had sex with or who my confidants are...umm, *they're confidants*)...and/or...and/or...and/or. I think because she was so controlling while I was growing up, that I was afraid to call her out on all of her boundary-breaking, and so, I would just grit my teeth and bear it as best as I could. I mean, it would only be a few days...what harm could it do?

Hmph. Famous last words. Those words almost always are.

OK, so again, because there was so much dysfunction between us, many times when she would come to Nashville, she would stay with a friend and I would just go and visit her over there. However, when it seemed like things were getting better between us, I eased into her staying at my place for a week; a week is pretty much my max with anyone (folks who know me know that my running statement is, "If you're not my husband, I'm not interested in a roommate."). That said, something that used to irk my mother is I never gave her my mailing address. I didn't do that because, again, boundaries, and I was right to be that way (more confirmation on that in a minute). However, because it did seem like things were getting better between us, whenever she would go out for a walk around my neighborhood, I didn't give it much thought. Health issues had always been a thing for her, and so, she was pretty "health intentional" — plus, she enjoyed nature. Oh, but a year later, I got what was *really* going on; how she *still* was trying to run my life on some level.

After some other things transpired that caused me to need to take some indefinite time off from our dynamic, about two weeks leading into the incident that I touched on during an earlier chapter, I found myself sleeping...A LOT. In fact, I was actually in the process of taking a nap when I heard banging on my door like there were some damn cops trying to get in. It was in the middle of the day and, again, I don't ever have many people know where I live, so everything about it seemed very odd. I called a friend to tell her what was going on and when I looked out of my bedroom window — there was my mother, staring at me like I was a three-year-old who was in trouble. Next to her was one of my now former spiritual mentors (because he violated my boundaries by even getting involved — he knew the deal; he had for years, so yes, that relationship had to end). *I couldn't believe it.* I intentionally didn't give you my address to avoid this kind of mess, and yet, here you are (in my 40s, no less). NO RESPECT FOR BOUND-ARIES — AGAIN.

When I did let her in, all she did was sit down and stare with the same kind look she used to give me when she was trying to intimidate me. It wasn't working, though. All I could feel was anger with a touch of disgust. I kept asking her what she wanted; she kept saying she simply needed to see me. No progress was being made. So, when I looked at my spiritual mentor and said, "This is so fucked up" and she responded with, "That's enough, Shellie!" — I lost it. No lie. You bogarted your way into my home, completely not invited on any level, and you're trying to tell me how to act?! You think that you are owed respect that you clearly didn't give...AGAIN? Yeah, you've got to go. I yelled, "Get out!" twice — and that is the last time that I've physically laid eyes on her.

A few weeks later, while hanging out at the same mall that I referred to in an earlier chapter (and will bring up again later on in this book), I ran into an older Black couple who was visiting from up north. After sharing some things that I felt impressed to say, the husband said, "It's clear that you are a prophet. Do you mind if we speak some things into your life too?" I didn't discern anything "off" about them (yes, you must discern who speaks into your life — even when it comes to family, by the way), so I said "yes". Two things he said were a trip. One was about the guy who is in an upcoming chapter about a nice guy narcissist. The gentleman said a name that was very close to his actual one (leaving that out for obvious reasons), then he said, "He knows that you are his soulmate but he will never mature enough to be a proper covering for you" (LISTEN). Then he said something about my mother: "Your mother recently came from overseas to visit you, right? She did not mean you well and I know you are upset with who brought her, but he actually protected you by being there." Hmph. That "mean you well" part? I edited it because what he actually said was far more jarring. Yep. That sealed it. Nothing but firm boundaries, moving forward. I know that I was given a messenger to confirm it in a very couldn't-deny-it-if-I-wanted-to kind of way. Oh, but my mother also came around and put an additional nail in the coffin, so to speak.

Several months later, a cousin on my mother's side became deathly ill. She emailed me updates. I said nothing. Then one day, out of the blue, I received an email from my molester. Whew, that man. He actually tried to dictate how I should handle the situation regarding my own family member. I don't know what was more *"Twilight Zone"* to me: him having the balls to contact me at all or my finding out, via him, that he knew how to because MY MOTHER and a so-called love aunt gave him my email address. The last straw? Although it should've been the guy in the mall, that right there was it. How unsafe can you be that, after all of these years, you are so desperate to get in contact with me, that you would give a supreme violator access to my life? Yeah, we're good — and done.

You know, something that I've made peace with is that when it comes to humanity, sometimes you are the student and sometimes you are the teacher. Then, sometimes, you are the lesson — for them. When it comes to people who railroad folks' boundaries, who refuse to take limits seriously, who just don't seem to ever shift and accept that they can't always have their way, sometimes the lesson they have to learn is a drastic one: *Sometimes you have to be willing to be their consequence because no one else is strong enough to do it.* And if that means losing you so that they can learn how to treat others better? If that is the "sacrificial lamb" of sorts that you've got to be...*so be it.*

Since all of this transpired (again, while I was in my 40s, so it wasn't a long time ago), I can't tell you how many people I've also had to shift away from because, while they were comfortable talking to me about how much even they didn't like my mother's "insistence" at times, they were too cowardly to tell her to her face. Since I seemed to be one of the only few to actually speak up and tell her how it is, that ended up having me look like the bad guy. What it also did was keep her from really learning how to stop trying to get people to do what she wanted them to so much. Others' lack of courage to truly confront her empowered her to rationalize that her controlling tendencies really weren't out of control — and *that* is why, once I removed myself from her, all of a sudden, I'm the extreme one when, really, had more people held her accountable, it quite possibly would have never even come to this. More and more, I get why God has no respect for cowards (again, Revelation 21:8). I don't either.

On this side of life, do I ever think that my mother and I will reconcile? The next to last chapter will touch on my thoughts on that word. For now, I'll just say that manipulating victims into doing more work than victimizers to make things right is some, as the social media folks say, really nasty work. That said, as far as reconciliation goes, I'm not totally against it; however, what I will NOT be doing is "returning to my own vomit again" (Proverbs 26:11). The days of not taking my "no" for an answer, treating me like I'm a child or trying to find ways to control what isn't yours to control are long gone and there is no wiggle room on that.

Do I miss her? I miss parts of her. *She's my mother.* However, I wouldn't trade the peace and healing that I now have for anything in the world. If that means us never speaking again, I am beyond prepared for that. What's a trip is, it's actually my mother who says that I am very violent about my peace and my healing. She would be correct. If you want to disrupt all of the work that I've done to have some consistency and sanity in my life, you've gotta go—person, place, thing or idea — including blood relatives.

To tell you the truth, the time apart has been revelatory in a myriad of different ways. For example, something else that I did over the past few years is set aside time to really unpack how and why so many of my past close female relationships ended up "mimicking" certain things about my dynamic with my mother — because, *we tend to do what's familiar, not what's right.* RIGHT? Until I removed that energy from my space, I didn't fully get how I ended up in such cyclic and sometimes damning situations, especially in comparison to what my intimate connections with women are like now.

And actually, that's where the title of this particular chapter comes in...

...

Because I was so used to being around a woman who was very pretty, super accomplished, seemed to speak in Scripture more than regular words most of the time, and because she was also very enigmatic in how she went about doing things, without even realizing it, I found myself gravitating toward and then choosing female friends who were very similar when it came to how they lived their own lives. Now, my first book? It talks about the worst female friend who I have ever had, to-date. She will always be the gold medal winner in that regard. At the same time, though, because again, until we heal — and it really can't be said enough that we really do tend to do what's familiar instead what's right — I want to show you how I kept repeating certain things about my mother and myself with other women, usually without even realizing it…until it was too late.

Do I have specific examples? *C'mon.* You've read enough of this book by now to *know* that I do. Again, I'm not using real names because of the mercy thing. I'm also doing it to throw nosy people off track (I keep using that word to trigger the ones who are — and my discernment knows that it's working. LOL). I'm big on name meanings, so I'm choosing to go with names that have similar, although not exact, meanings to their real ones (two points for creativity). I'm also going to leave origin stories out; no need for those.

Felicity. Felicity has always been beautiful, although she never really fully knew it, because I don't think that her parents really affirmed her in that way; that's my mother, for sure. And although Felicity and I rarely had any conflict, I could never fully exhale in her space either. Even she once told me that she doesn't know if she knows how to do intimacy well with anyone, and I would totally agree with her self-assessment. I think a part of the reason was because, although her family is full of believers, there was also a ton of mental illness (some diagnosed, some not) up in there, so it was like Felicity had walls up to protect herself from her own people, which means that you never really could get to know her, fully. Maybe that's why she had such a sneaky side to her — one that she didn't really take a lot of accountability for. Somehow, some way, it was going to be someone else's fault for why she did some of the foul things that she did. She also really sucked at apologizing. Eight times out of ten, she was going to take the justifying or deflecting route, even if it ultimately got her absolutely nowhere — and that was draining. Ultimately, what caused us to shift is she had no problem with you investing emotionally more in her than she did in you, and that led her to not really valuing our friendship. If I was willing to do most of the work to keep us going, so be it. If I stopped and that resulted in us no longer being close or friends, she was fine with that too. In short, Felicity kept me codependent. And codependency between my mother and I existed in abundance.

Adriel. I don't think I realized just how narcissistic Adriel was until I had finally had enough — enough of her wanting to talk more than listen; enough of her using me when her other friendships were disappointing her; enough of how entitled she could be; enough of spending literally thousands on her when, after years of us being friends, I can't think of one gift that I ever received that had an actual price tag on it — *not one*; enough of doing things to help her career when I can't name one way that she helped mine (and she had connections, just as I did); enough of her picking and choosing when I should be relevant in her life based on the hierarchy that was in her mind (at any given time); enough of her emotional instability; enough of her humble bragging (she did that incessantly); enough of her deflecting responsibility when I would bring things up to her that were foul on her part

— just…ENOUGH. Adriel was super subtle in her narcissism, though. She would come off as syrupy sweet and complimentary, almost as if to make you feel guilty for calling her out on her ish. Yet more than any of this, two things that got me to the point and place of being *done* done was her weaponizing my relationship with someone else in her life in a way that we truly will never come back from as well as her only seeming to be present when things were bad instead of good in my world. It's like she was an emotional ambulance chaser in the sense that it made her feel good about herself to have to "fix", "save" or "rescue" you; when I was good, though, we really didn't have a lot to talk about. A lot of spiritual narcissists enjoy playing Holy Ghost, Jr. I grew up with that energy, so it took me a while to catch on as far as Adriel was concerned.

Deva. Talented and hella emotionally unstable. That was Deva in a nutshell. And honestly, although I never really wanted to admit it to myself, after some others brought it to my attention, I think there was some low-key envy that was always going on too. On one hand, she, like Adriel, would be overly-complimentary, flattering, even. On the other, it's like she would get mad out of nowhere that I didn't make some of the life choices that she did. In a nutshell, Deva was quite unpredictable and that was exhausting. Even when she knew that she was in the wrong about something, she would find a way to play the victim and punish *you* for the pain that *she* caused — and a lot of pain came from dealing with her because of this. In some ways, I'm also the most grateful for our interaction because she was the first person who, after doing some really mean and vindictive stuff and coming back around, pretty much like it never happened, and I was like, "Yeah…I think I'm good" — that taught me that I could deeply care about someone and still know that I need to leave them alone…because when people are that calculated in how they handle things, there is a dark side of them that you typically should keep your distance from. Yeah, that was another thing about Deva: She seemed to constantly have dark energy in her space, which always led to some pretty bizarre spiritual battles. That is definitely something that I felt my mother went through. I knew/know she loves God, yet sometimes, she would say and do things that were very…contrary to that…at the most unexpected times.

Kaina. At least at the time when we were friends, Kaina was a liar. I mean, a bona fide pathological one. It wasn't even malicious; it just seemed to be a part of who she was — a literal alter ego. If I made the time to psychoanalyze why, I would say that a lot of it had to do with some of the trauma in her own childhood, her profession and always gravitating to churches that told her what to think instead of encouraging her to develop a mind of her own. I also believe that since she was praised for her looks more than her character, she invested more in the former than the latter. I won't lie — there are a lot of things about Kaina that I've always liked; I just could never fully trust her because, while she would try and "convict me" for choices that I made, she would constantly "get busted" for things that were at least three times as destructive (especially self-destructive), and that caused me to get to a point and place where I really couldn't trust her. Plus, she kind of used me. I was the friend who had to listen to all of her issues while another friend was the one who she rewarded with outings, trips and gifts. It was almost like this weird secret lover thing minus the sex. Our final straw, though, was telling me her something that she didn't want to hear: She had a pattern for picking the wrong men and having cyclic dynamics with them. She "punished me" for that by rescinding our friendship. Word on the street is that my discernment turned out to be spot-on, though. Anyway, the "I-like-you-yet-can't-really-trust-you-because-you-like-to-project-your-sneaky-shit-onto-me-perhaps-so-I-won't-catch-on-to-you?" That's what she "mimicked" the most when it comes to me and my mom. I was told that I was a liar a lot. Meanwhile, I was consistently finding out…strange things about the person who was saying that. (Projecting much?)

Sanira. A wise person once said that most people don't want advice unless you're going to agree with what they already think or you're going to tell them what they want to hear. That is Sanira in a nutshell. She would constantly come to me for insight, then want to debate what I thought, do her own thing, and then get upset with me when things went the way that I predicted that it would in the first place (mostly because I started to peep her pattern). In fact, I think it's absolutely amazing that the main thing that "offended" her still ended up manifesting. She started having feelings for a guy who showed signs of disrespect toward her, right out the gate. When I told her that, in spite of her wanting to be a wife and have children, he was not going to give her a family, she got upset with me, stayed with him anyway, and, to this day, she's *still* not a wife and still has no kids. Hearing what she wants to hear and then acting like life gave her what she chose, when it actually was *her* who was constantly romanticizing cyclic decisions — I was so used to living in that kind of emotional environment while growing up. Everything ain't Satan, chile. A lot of stuff is straight up…YOU.

I'm sure that being a writer is a big part of the reason why I'm recommending what I'm about to say, yet all of this is why I'm a huge fan of what I call "relationship journaling." Sometimes, taking out moments to jot down your own relational patterns can illuminate some things that you wouldn't see any other way. For me, once I started really processing my patterns with past female relationships, especially as it related to what my dynamic with my mother had been like, I then found myself in friendships that were more stable, steady and accountable — in both directions. I wasn't choosing people who caused me to be there for them more than they were there for me, who hid behind spirituality to avoid confrontation or who wouldn't know accountability if it socked them dead in the face. I wasn't settling for people who tried to make me feel like I was the unpopular girl in high school who got picked by the cheerleading squad (you know, the kind of folks who wanted fans more than friends). I didn't find myself gravitating to those who took more than they gave — relationally, monetarily, or otherwise. My female relationships now are healthy, balanced and safe. *Very safe*. And, in turn, due to that circle of mutual accountability and trust, that has made me a safer person to be around too.

You know, we tend to spend a lot of time talking about how fathers set the tone for how daughters see men in romantic dynamics, yet more needs to be said about how mothers set the tone for the kind of female friendships that daughters lean into as well.

For me, there used to be so much "fear in love"...and I get why.

These days, healthy love has cast out all fear.

To the women who have made this happen for me, I salute you.

To the women who taught me how to intimately avoid others like them, I thank you.

"In order to create your future,
you have to reconcile your past."

(JOHN TARNOFF)

Chapter Six

My Children. And Their Fathers. A Reflective Recap.

If you're a skimmer more than a reader and/or you never read my first book, the bottom line with this chapter is, I had four abortions in the 90s (the first at 19 and the rest in my 20s). I wasn't aggressive or intentional about getting pregnant in my thirties; I decided that if I didn't conceive a child by my early 40s, I wasn't going to have any children at all — and I didn't. And now, I'm on the tail end of perimenopause (chile…CHILE). Oh, and as far as the "three-and-a-possible" men who I once conceived children with? They are all fathers now. There it all is in a nutshell. And you know what? Surprisingly, I'm at peace with all of this. If I'm really gonna be all the way real, in many ways, I'm floored by just how at peace I am…which causes me to wonder if I ever really wanted children to begin with.

I mean, we're all grown, so let me be totally candid: No matter where you stand on the abortion topic, I think we all can agree that four terminations are a bit excessive. And even though I know that I didn't want to get pregnant by the last boyfriend that I will ever have in this lifetime (even though we didn't always have sex like I felt that way; so glad that life also agreed), and the journey with the nice guy narcissist (who we will tackle very soon) took up virtually all of my 30s, if I *really wanted* to have a child, I could've — hell, and should've. Yet I didn't. On this side of looking back, I think there are a few reasons why things have played out the way that they did.

For one thing, when it came to my own upbringing, I often say that if my mother and my brother's father (who was around in the home until I was about 15) were given old-school report cards for their parenting skills, they were either handed As or straight-up Fs — nothing really in between. And honestly, the A's were good enough that I considered parenting, yet the F's were so damn traumatizing that a part of me was always afraid that, on some level and in some way, I would subject my own kids to the same extreme roller coaster ride that I endured due to them both.

Another reason is — well, I'll put it to you this way: There's a platonic friend in my life who has never been married, has no children, makes six figures, and, up until recently, has always worked in the nonprofit world dealing with youth. He's in his 40s now and when he told me that he didn't want kids because he feels like he has "parented all of Nashville", in many ways, I got where he was coming from. For several years, I was a teen mom director for the local chapter of a Christian-based nonprofit, and although that experience helped to heal me in ways that I didn't even know that I needed (because at the time, many of the teen moms I mentored were as old as my children would've been had I not terminated my pregnancies), and although working with them is exactly why I decided to become a doula (anyone who's done even a little bit of Googling about Black women and their mortality rates due to pregnancy can totally read between the lines there), dealing with those girls and all that came with them was a lot...*definitely* one of the best unconventional forms of birth control that I ever had. Indeed, if you're going to be a parent, you have to be super present. My bandwidth? I'm not sure if I had it fully for a "24/7-until-death-parts-me-from-my-offspring" kind of thing. At the age of 49, with perimenopausal signs getting louder by the day, I guess we'll never know.

Still another reason is, it takes a helluva lot of courage to hear what basically every parent (who is actually listening to their children; a lot of parents truly suck at doing that) will, at least 20 times, say before they leave this earth: "You messed up. And not just a little bit either." Listen, between my friends and my clients, I am constantly watching some people who thought that they did a stellar job when it came to raising their kids, find themselves damn near close to being mortified once their children reveal an attitude of, "Eh, not so much" — *and that* has been like a totally painful gut punch, not just to their ego but the core of their very essence and being. I don't know if I have the wherewithal to endure that because, sometimes the level of "mess up" that parents have done, it has literally altered their children, including grown children, in some pretty significant, if not flat-out damning ways — ways that some folks never fully bounce back or recover from.

And then there's the abstinence thing. Let's just say that the longer you go without sex, the pickier you become, and although all of my former baby daddies are, for the most part, pretty solid men (especially now), for me to engage in unprotected sex again, the caliber of guy would have to increase — significantly and exponentially so. Otherwise, what's the point? The season of abstinence was for absolute naught.

Now back to my babies' daddies (I mean, that *is* what they are... right?). Let's talk about those guys for just a moment since they did get a fair amount of writing space in my first read. Interestingly enough, some years back, I wrote an article about what a day in my life would've been like had I kept all four of my children. It's entitled "1993, 1994, 1997 and 1999"; I'm pretty sure you can guess why. Although it's clearly fictionalized, I did name my kids and I still refer to them with those names, even outside of the piece. The year 1993 is Damien; it means "to tame" (no, it does not mean "the devil" or "the Antichrist"; *The Omen* is just a movie). The year 1994 is Ava; it means "like a bird". The year 1997 is Nasya; it means "miracle of God". And the year 1999 is Solomon; it means "peace". The reason why I went through this, surprisingly healing exercise, is because, while I don't exactly wish that I had four children in the here and now, as I've spiritually evolved in many ways, I do recognize how selfish the decision to terminate was in the sense of me taking it upon myself to decide someone's ultimate fate: to determine that their purpose wasn't as valid as mine, simply because they would be "an inconvenience" in my world and/or I was afraid that I wouldn't know what to do with them… had I had them.

Walking by faith, not by sight (2 Corinthians 5:7) was not something that I had the courage to do in this particular area; at least, not at the time. And while we're here, I think it's important to put on record that when it comes to faith — at least the biblical definition of *"Now faith is the substance of things hoped for, the evidence of things not seen"* (Hebrews 11:1—NKJV) — a definition of hope to keep in mind is "the feeling that what is wanted can be had that events will turn out for the best" — one or the other, not both, y'all. A lot of times, we make some truly irresponsible and/or selfish decisions because we think that faith means that things should always go how we want them to when, oftentimes, we need to just trust that, ultimately, if we fully surrender to God's will, things will ultimately turn out for the best (Romans 8:28).

Anyway, when I went to the Creator of both myself and those children (because the Bible says that the fruit of *the womb* is a reward — Psalm 127:3) about how I can even scratch the surface of how to make an amends for aborting (because when you're truly repentant for something, you should do your best to make an amends for the wrong that you did and/or the havoc that you caused), not just my seed but their purpose on this planet, the instruction that the Spirit (John 4:24) gave me was to prayerfully select their names and then intentionally live out the meanings of those names, every day, until my last breath. And that's just what I've done. By doing so, it has restored me in ways that I will never be able to fully put into words. In fact, I actually have a tattoo that's in honor of my children. No, that part of my past has not escaped me. I have made the decision to make sure that it never does.

You know, I've shared, many times, on a variety of platforms, that my last abortion was December 4, 1999. That is a whopping 25 years ago, which means that my youngest would've been (wow) 24 years of age at this point. Since all of my other children were older, it also completely blows my mind that I could've very easily been a grandmother by now. And whenever people ask me how I am able to speak so freely about all of this, my answer is pretty much the same: I know that I've been forgiven — not just by God but the spirit of those babies too. Why do I say that? Mostly, it's because I have a very, well, let's go with "strange" relationship with children I don't know. Random kids will clap for me in the mall. Toddlers will point, wave and laugh. I can't tell you how many parents have looked at me like, "How do you know my child?" when their son or daughter will walk up to hold an impromptu conversation with me. I can't do anything about what I've done in my past, yet I do think that because I am not dismissive, nonchalant or flippant about it now is why those little tiny messengers are sure to let me know that they think that I'm a safe space. And to them, for making the time to do that, I am eternally grateful. Like, tearing-up-as-I'm-typing-this grateful.

Something else that has aided in my healing is the fact that I now have two (technically three but that's another story for another time) goddaughters: Grace and Nova. At the time that this book is published, Grace is 13 and Nova is five. When their mother first asked me to be Grace's godmom, it took me an entire year to give her an official "yes". The main reason is because I have two sets of godparents and they all absolutely sucked at the gig — to this day, they still do. I don't recall a birthday present, a graduation attendance or gift. When my books came out, they didn't acknowledge it. A few years back, my "second godmother" asked me to meet her and all I did was watch her shop all day (which I thought was pretty rude) and then, when we went to lunch, she basically did a commercial for my mother and why I should tolerate certain things that I was starting not to — and that was after saying that she felt that she wasn't really asked to be my godmother to begin with; that she was basically told to do it, which made me think that was her agenda all along (to meet with me to tell me that). And then, a couple of years after that, she sent a series of gaslighting emails with selective memory about that entire interaction (le sigh). So yeah, all that to say, I definitely didn't want any kids to look at me like I see my own godparents; therefore, I needed a minute to make sure that I could and would truly rise to the occasion. According to my godbabies' mom, I think I might be more involved than she thought that I would be (LOL). Yeah, those are my girls (we're all Geminis and everything!). I'm in it for the long haul. Y'all who accept the godparent-ing role, it's about more than wearing matching outfits with parents on the day when their kids are getting blessed. If you're not going to *fully* commit, for the rest of those children's lives, please just politely decline. I know a lot of people who are scarred, to this day, because their godparents didn't take their job seriously. For shame too because the title literally has the word "god" in it. GOODNESS.

OK, so with all of that out of the way, if you're curious about what my babies' daddies have been up to, here ya go:

Damien's father is David in my first book. Lawd, that man. Anyway, let me first just give the update. Ironically, he is now a father to four of his own children: three girls and one boy. After years of being in and out of prison, he's now a business owner of a thriving company, an impressive dad and an adolescent (LOL) believer. David and I? We've always had a weird thing between us. The reason why I say that is because, over the past 20 years, we've had run-ins. One time, in partic-ular, I went over to his apartment to watch *The Notebook* (chile, what was I thinking?!). After it, we were kissing and disrobing and then, out of nowhere, he literally picked me up and put me out of his apartment. He told me through the door that "he couldn't handle" the intimacy between us; that if we weren't married, he didn't think that we should be sexually active anymore. At the time, it felt like rejection. In real time, I get that it was love. Anyway, what's wild is, right up until I was penning this book, I thought I would be speaking of him solely in past tense because, although first loves are damn near impossible to shake off, I really thought that our chapter was totally and completely done. Oh, but me and that man, chile. Long story short, one day, I had an urge for some veal from Carrabba's — a restaurant that I hadn't been to in literal years. When I arrived, I found myself conflicted about going there or to another restaurant that was several feet way. I decided on the latter, and, as I was thoroughly enjoying my lamb chops, here he comes walking in the front door. Thirty-plus years in, this man still makes my heart jump (again, first loves are powerful!). Anyway, as he told the identical story of trying to decide which restaurant to walk into and also told me that it was "fancy meeting me that day" because he just left court to get officially off of parole from poor decisions that were made oh so many years ago...let's just say that at the time of me penning this, there has been some talking, along with some healing and definitely a lot of clarity that has manifested. It's different now than it was when he was 15 (have mercy!) and I was almost 19. Now it's 47 and 50. Most of his kids are grown. We both have made peace with the loss of our dads. For the most part, we both are happy as individuals. Neither of us have ever been married. We both want to know why we can't seem to let each other go — and why the universe makes sure that never happens. Honestly, I don't know what else to tell y'all other than, as my inner circle says, "This is such a signature Shellie kind of thing" — and they would be spot-on with that assess-ment. Damien's father is my "love alpha". Is he my "omega"? In the wise words of DeBarge, time will reveal. All I know is a sistah went in looking for some lamb chops and came out with what very well may be another book someday. One way or another. For now, what I will say is I have emotionally matured in the sense that I know a part of my attachment is consequences of him being my first love and the fact that he has a lot of characteristics of my father. This means that sometimes, we need time to see what's real vs. what's simply...con-sequences. I've chosen to let time make the ultimate call. I'm living my life as I did before we ran into each other (again) in the meantime. And there is some real healing and freedom in just saying that — and meaning it.

Ava's father. In some ways, in all candor, it's a bit of a toss-up between my first love and first lust as far as who her dad *actually* is. I shared in my first book that this is the case because I was having semi-regular sex with who I called "my first lust" and then impulsive sex with my first love. Then, if you add that I found out I was 13 weeks after my abortion, when I thought that I was around eight (please don't assume that your period is always a pregnancy predictor; if you had unprotected sex, *always take a test*) — I'll just say that deep down, I believe my Damien's father is Ava's dad too; however, just to cover all of the bases, my first lust is a father as well. He is actually the oldest of the four men, the last to become a dad, and, quite frankly, he's the one who was the hardest for me to hear the news about (by the way, I heard the news from him in the form of an email; yes, we're in a good space). Mostly because, after my third abortion, my mother said, "These men are going to go on to have children and you're not going to have any." I don't know if that was a threat, a curse or what, however, that's just the way that it played out. I can't say that the sole reason for why I ended my pregnancies was "for the men" yet I will say that if you find yourself in the position that I was in back in my 20s, think long and hard about doing it just because some dude wants you to. Their life goes on and I don't recall getting a thank-you card, email or text from any of those jokers about the sacrifice that I made in order for their lives to be easier. SMDH. Anyway, Ava's (potential) father and I are cool, in a very cool way. Becoming a father at almost 50 (at the time) was wild for me to process. Fatherhood does look good on him, though. Congrats.

Nasya's dad. Yeah, he's a trip. Even years into him getting married, he would periodically email me about still wanting to have some sort of a sexual relationship. It's interesting because, out of the four men, we probably would've been the best co-parents because our values are somewhat similar and, at his core, he's a nice guy — not the kindest man yet nice. What's the difference? Nice can be performative and conditional. Kind is about being genuinely good and benevolent (I'll get more into that breakdown in another chapter). It's funny because, sometimes I will see him on television; he pops up at the most random of times, and yet, I'm not surprised at all. When it's all said and done, he turned out just like I thought he would: successful, a family man, basically a posterchild for wholesome Blackness. Good for him. He's two kids in. There's no love lost on any level. I just learned to block his email address since, although I helped him to "cheat" on his girlfriend, I have absolutely no desire to assist with helping him to also cheat on his wife.

And finally, Solomon's father. We were very close friends once upon a time. He said that, even though he was attracted to me, we shouldn't have sex. I didn't see that as protection of our relationship at the time; again, it felt more like rejection, so I pushed to do it anyway — just like I pushed for sex without a condom a few times because I delusionally thought that it made me "special". He ultimately resented me for that and the pregnancy (although, clearly, he did it — yeah, *exactly*). I saw him and raised him by having an abortion and resenting him. Anyway, I'm sure it's no shocker that he moved on and got someone else pregnant a year later. Years later, that story earned me my first national byline in a major publication. As life would have it, his mom and I remained close for years. For the most part, that made him uncomfortable because his baby mama-turned-wife was livid about it. Strangely enough, around the same time that I heard that he was ending his marriage, his mom and I had a very bizarre con-versation (on her part) that led me to the conclusion that our season was up. As far as kids go, Solomon's dad only had one child (although he helped her to raise some of her other children). I don't know what I think or how I feel about him. He's the one who I am the least inter-ested in as far as "So, what are you up to now" goes. Not because I'm mad. I'm just...done.

And what do I feel about all of the fathers as a whole? I think I'm just amazed that men can seem to have kids for, hell, ever (one of my friends actually has a toddler sister and he's in his 50s!). Maybe that's why some of them can be so nonchalant, aloof or even reckless when they ask women to get on top of sterile tables to get their seed vacuumed out of their wombs. I guess my follow-up thought to that is folks really need to read *TIME* magazine's article, "How Previous Sexual Partners Affect Offspring". Yeah, when you get a chance, Google that bad boy. Folks like to think that casual sex has no consequences or that aborting a child removes all evidence that the baby ever existed. WRONG. Science says that when you conceive a child with someone, their DNA remains a part of you on some level. Hmph. I wonder if those guys ever considered that I may have influenced the outcome of the children who they now have. Sex is serious. SEX. IS. SERIOUS. Finally, I think my last thought is, I know what the fallout for listening to them when they asked me to abort has been like on my end; sometimes, I am curious what life has been for them, though. It took two people to get pregnant, two people made the decision to terminate — this means that two people also have lasting consequences. I will say that when it comes to my first love, he has articulated, many times over, that he still struggles with fully forgiving me because he believes that it's his other children who truly saved his life and, if I had kept his first child, perhaps he would've made better decisions sooner. See...

choices always have a rippling effect. We must choose wisely. As for the other fathers, maybe one day I'll ask for their thoughts. We'll see.

In the meantime, sometimes, when I'm being interviewed, I'll be asked if I'm angry with those men, if I want to get back at them or if I feel like they gypped me in some way. I am not and do not. With a 20-plus year look back on it all, I'll just say this: Sex while you're single tends to be a very selfish act and outcomes like an unwanted/ unplanned pregnancy puts that fact totally on front street. And so, if you don't want to take the risk of the potentially devastating consequences that come with participating in an act that tends to take an "every man and woman for themselves" turn when the going gets tough…DON'T DO IT.

Lives are on the line. Legacies are on the line. YOU ARE ON THE LINE.

Full stop and period.

…

Oh, and as far as some of the other characters that I had sex with and a child did not come out of the "exchange", I can sum them up by saying that most of them are married, from what I hear (and sometimes see), around 60 percent of them appear to be happily so — and in between my first book and this one, I did go on what I call a "Get Your Heart Pieces Back" tour, of sorts, because I needed to remove certain titles from some of them in my mind like "the one who got away" or "the one I wish I had married". Long story short, all of that worked out for my good, and while I can't change the past or connection that I shared with any of those individuals, other than my first love, no one really "gets to me"….anymore. A long season of abstinence played a role in that. Taking off the lust-laden, rose-colored glasses on some of them played a role in that. Learning how to separate how someone makes you feel vs. who they actually are played a role in that. And shoot, time, period, played a role in that. Purge. Release. Peace. That's it in a nutshell.

All is well. For those who genuinely care...thanks for asking (well...wondering).

Oh, and if you are someone who read my first book and is thinking, "Damn, that one talked about sex a lot while this one barely seems to be", that would be an accurate assessment — 10 points for you. LOL. Last time, I talked about what was relevant in my life at the time, and this time is no different.

Either you caught that or...you didn't. I'm fine either way.

*"The minute you settle for less than you deserve,
you get even less than you settled for."*

(MAUREEN DOWD)

Chapter Seven

No More Boyfriends. I'm Too Old for a "Boy" Anything.

So, are you saying that you regret us being together? The last boyfriend who I will ever have in this lifetime asked me that a few years ago, during a multi-hour phone conversation — one that he claimed he needed to have with me in order to get some things off of his chest.

"Yes. We should've never dated. We should've just remained friends." That was my immediate reply.

Having regrets. Personally, I don't trust people who claim that they don't have any regrets in life. It's mostly because, being the word-literal person that I am, I know that regret means remorse, and if any human is walking around here professing to not feel some sort of "deep and painful regret for wrongdoing" for things that have said or done before, they A) totally suck at personal accountability (which a lot of people do); B) are narcissistic as hell, and/or C) are complete and total sociopaths.

And just why do I have so much remorse as it relates to my final ex-boyfriend? Shit, where do I begin?

For starters, I come from a long line of both men and women who, as religious and Bible-toting as they claim to be, have been married multiple times. Although I think there is definitely some lack of personal accountability and the confusion of mercy vs. grace going on when it comes to their justifications for having several spouses in their lifetime, let them tell it, a big part of the reason why they jumped — or is it rode (LOL) — so many brooms are because they were pressured to not cancel their weddings. Instead, they were convinced that there was more humiliation in calling their nuptials off than getting into something that had red flags all over it right out the gate. For me, the way that ended up manifesting in my own life is interesting because, again, my ex and I were really good friends before we became more than that. I found him to be brilliant, gifted and funny—I was never really attracted to him, though. Oh, but amidst the presents, love letters and songs that he had written for/about me, well...our origin story is that I recall riding in my car one day, letting him drive it (him driving *my car* was pretty much the reality of *our dynamic* which is another regret that I'll get into in a sec), looking over at him and thinking, "I *guess* that I can give it a shot." Lawd. He didn't deserve my thinking that way and I didn't deserve to settle in that fashion either. Regret.

Another regret is I had already messed with (and by "messed with", I mean "slept with") a relative of his — one who, when he asked me if it was true that I was dating his family member and I said yes, his immediate response was, "Good luck. My family is crazy." When I laughed, he said, "I'm not kidding." *He's not kidding.* The amount of unusual, bizarre, nonsensical, chaotic and straight-up foolish things that I've had a second if not front-row seat to when it comes to so many people in that bloodline, even in real time, as easily as 75 percent of them find themselves throwing Scriptures around like it's confetti in order to deflect from or delusionally justify their own mess? It is completely off the charts. Even many of the family members talk about how crazy each other are, almost like it's an Olympic sport. Dodging a bullet by not having myself officially attached to all of that — the entire family tree, not just my ex's — is a complete and total understatement. In fact, when a former spiritual mentor asked me to break down the traits of my now-ex-then-boyfriend-at-the-time and I said, "He's very sweet and smart. His family is crazy but…" and my mentor said, "Oh, so he's the *least* crazy of the crew then?" — I wish I had taken that more to heart. Over the years, since we've been broken up, I've found out some, let's go with hella cryptic ways, about how even he moves. DNA has commonalities in it, especially if people don't seek professional help to break certain predispositions, patterns or habits that run within the bloodline. Hell, I can personally attest to that. Hell again, that's a huge part of what this book is all about.

Another regret? Allowing *his* issues to become *my* problem. I don't mean being compassionate or sympathetic towards him — I mean that I easily bankrolled 90 percent of that relationship. I won't get into all of the reasons why; however, what I will share is that while, for his 25th birthday, I rented out a theatre and played his favorite film for him and his loved ones and friends, I don't recall ever receiving a birthday or Christmas gift while we dated. Him not having money? Uh-huh, birthdays and holidays don't move around; this means that you have a rotating 364 days to come up with some sort of plan, sir. Meanwhile, according to him, he was too "traumatized" to be thoughtful in that way due to growing up with money, life life-ing in his home during his teenage years, and him deciding that to not expect anything from or really doing anything for others? That was his way of coping. *So, I had to suffer because of your shit?* That's selfish as hell.

Still another regret? WASTED TIME. We were together for four years and then kept having sex for two years after that, mostly because a breakup often comes in phases. Indeed, as the old song says, "breaking up is hard to do". It's kind of crazy to process that the last time I recall ever sleeping with him, I was 32. We're five years apart (he's five years younger than I am which is another thing that several women in my family have a tendency to do: get with younger men — sometimes much younger men; my mother's third husband is 15 years younger than she is), we started dating almost 19 years ago, stopped having sex 17 years ago — and yet, here I am, 49, and *still healing* from some of the regrets from this particular chapter of my life.

So, what am I ultimately saying? Was it all just one big ball of regret? The relationship? In many ways, absolutely. Knowing him? No. Although nothing about who I am today would ever consider something beyond a platonic connection with my ex, I was such an emotional wreck due to so much of what I've already addressed in this here book of mine that, at the time, he seemed like a consummate equalizer. In other words, I had so much pain, fear and low self-esteem that manifested in so many ways back then, that A) a lot of the red, orange and even yellow flags that I saw about him; B) the fact that I was the one doing most of the work that traditionally guys do in romantic relationships, and C) the reality of me thinking that settling was the best that I deserved because "something" is better than nothing at all — I just kept ignoring it...year, after year, after year. Years that I can never, ever, get back. Lord, do I regret that.

And just why would I put myself (and him) through that? Why would I allow what was so...holistically counterproductive? A huge part of the reason is because it is my very firm opinion that our culture (including church culture) absolutely sucks when it comes to dating.

It's a book series, podcast and TED Talk to get into all of the reasons why that is the case, yet I will tackle one. Our culture likes boyfriends and girlfriends to move in their dynamic as if they are already married. No, you can't talk to other members of the opposite sex on the cell phone that *you* pay the bills on because that would be "cheating". Yes, you should push through all of the things that you either don't like or aren't working because you are in a committed relationship. And Lord, if I hear one more person say that women should submit to men while dating them (single women owe *femininity* not *submission*). *Please be quiet.* Submission is, largely in part, a biblical concept and it's very clear that it's for *married couples only* (Colossians 3:18, Ephesians 5:22–24, Titus 2:5). In fact, don't even get me started on the reality that there is not one Scripture that even references boyfriends and girlfriends. NOT. ONE. Yet, before coming into really accepting all of this for myself, I felt that I deserved my now-ex the type of loyalty and devotion that comes with being a wife. I. DID. NOT. Words cannot express just how deeply I regret not accepting that very real fact sooner.

So, what was the final straw that ended things? I mean, *really* ended them? I was at the house of a relative of his and I was just… miserable. Although I knew that the relationship was no longer serving me, pretty much at all, at the same time, I couldn't act like I wasn't so, well, used to him being in my life that the idea of him no longer being a part of it (because he had always made it crystal clear that he burns bridges with exes; I'm not sure if that was a threat or not, looking back) wasn't a bit terrifying. In fact, when I called him from that home and told him that we needed to be *done* done, after I hung up, I balled up in a corner and cried — no, I sobbed. I don't even remember when I got up. Hell, I can't tell you when I stopped crying either.

I do know that those first 3-6 months were extremely difficult. I guess I liken it to a type of detox. And even that is a red flag. I shouldn't feel like breaking up with a man, especially a man who I was never fully into, is basically like coming off of a drug — yet when you feel like you need to feel needed more than you want to be loved in a healthy and thorough kind of way, things can find themselves being just that toxic. Unfortunately so. And yet, interestingly enough, one thing that I don't regret? A quote that I now carry very close to me that serves as the main reason why I will never find myself in the position that I was in with my final ex-boyfriend, with a boyfriend, any boyfriend, ever again:

"As soon as the love relationship does not lead me to me, as soon as I in a love relationship do not lead another person to himself, this love, even if it seems to be the most secure and ecstatic attachment I have ever experienced, is not true love. For real love is dedicated to continual becoming." (Leo Buscaglia)

Why get into a relationship with someone who you already know is going to hinder you from becoming the best version of yourself? And definitely why stay one moment longer once you discover that your growth has become stagnant...or that you are going backward? Yeah, that's another problem with dating like you're married: You stop remembering that *you are your top priority* (under God, of course) when that is *exactly* how you should move (you being your top priority). You forget that, as I oftentimes say, until/unless your taxes say that you are married, single you remain — it doesn't matter how long you've been seeing someone. "Dating" is not a relational status when it comes to the Good Book or the IRS.

That said, if there's one thing that I get asked, fairly often, especially since I am a sex and relationships writer and marriage life coach, it's how have I been comfortable with not having at least a boyfriend for all of these years. Well, to be honest with you, the chapter following this will explain some of what I ended up doing with a chunk of my time "in between men" (SMDH). However, aside from that and amidst all of the regret, if there is a silver lining — a beauty for ashes, if you will — in all of this, it's the fact that I get that a boyfriend should never be a husband hybrid; instead, I would prefer to have male friends, and, should one of those friendships transform itself into a relationship at some point...all good.

And boy, have I found so much joy and freedom in living this way because, as one of my male friends said to me not too long ago, "Shellie, you really do have a lot of male friends. It's kind of wild." He's right. Know what else is amazing? Listen, don't blame me that pop culture refers to men who make six figures, are at least six feet tall and are blessed to have at least six inches (now that last part, I don't know about when it comes to the male friends in my life — LOL) to be the "6-6-6 man"; however, I would say that easily 95 percent of the men who are my homies fit that bill. They are all attractive, ambitious, kind, generous, supportive, very real with me (I definitely need that type of energy and accountability) and supremely loyal. They're protective of me and my heart too. I dunno, ever since relinquishing the concept of boyfriends and embracing having genuine and *nonsexual* friendships (because if you read my first book, you may recall that my pattern was oftentimes sleeping with friends), I really haven't felt the need or desire to have a boyfriend. I mean, either I'm going to be your wife or I'm going to be your friend; all of that in-between ish? Y'all can have it. It's complicated. It's messy. It's a poor man's substitute for marriage. Yeah, I'm good on all-a-dat.

Not to mention the fact that the word "boyfriend" sounds ridiculous once you're actually grown. I mean, it's so crazy the things that society does simply because it's what everyone else is doing. A boy, by definition, is a male child. A boy, by definition, is also "a young man who lacks maturity, judgment, etc.". Chile, and maybe that's why the Bible never mentions a boyfriend (or girlfriend) anywhere in it — because marriage is for adults and it makes absolutely no sense to be out here trying to consider pledging forever to an individual who is immature, lacks discernment and does all of the other things that children tend to do.

Now does the title of this chapter make sense? Not only is my almost-50-butt too old for a "boy" anything, I have gone through too much blood, sweat and tears out here, yes literally, to be acting like a wife to someone who I am not actually married to. I have matured out of that notion. We can be cool, we can be friends, we can be friends until something grows into engagement — or we can be…nothing. However, it plays out, I'm at peace all the way around. Promise you that.

And what if all of this means that I never end up getting married? Although I'll get more into this in another chapter, and also even though everything about my purpose is almost hilariously relationally covenant-based, I'm honestly OK with that as well. If there are two things that I am unapologetically and unwaveringly customized for, it's a Black man (I'm not debating or defending that, there is absolutely no need) and covenant — and marriage is a covenant not some doggone boyfriend. If it's not right, I don't want it. If that means never having it, I'm at peace.

So, now you *really* get why this chapter has the title that it does, don't you?

No more regretting boyfriends.

No need to regret what you no longer want, need or…do. #Elmoshrug

"Some people play victims
of crimes they committed."
(UNKNOWN)

Chapter Eight

The Nice Guy Narcissist
(Whew, Chile)

Being a writer means that I do a lot of research (because I like people to walk away actually learning something, not merely being entertained). That said, kudos to a woman by the name of Tonya Lester, LCSW who once penned an article for *Psychology Today* entitled, "How to Handle a 'Kind' Narcissist" because, interestingly enough, I "found" it (is anything ever just happenstance…I mean, really?) weeks after I came up with this particular title. Anyway, her piece is all about detecting some of the subtleties of certain types of narcissists and, when it comes to a kind one, her very first paragraph said, "The kind narcissist sees themselves as a good person. Often, they appear steady and good-natured. They are popular and well thought of. The trouble arises once more is asked of them than they want to give."

Lawd. LAWD.

Now, before we get all up and into this particular chapter, two things: One, if there is a part of you that is like, "There sure are a lot of narcissists up in this book", I would agree. So much, in fact, that I asked my therapist friend, along with some of my accountability partners, if they thought that I may be in denial about being one myself.

Therapist friend: "Although every human has some narcissistic traits, you are definitely on the low end. I do think that a lot of your relationships have been extreme at times and the endings have been abrupt because you dealt with narcissists and didn't initially realize it. Probably because of the heavy religious environment that you grew up in and the fact that you came up in the entertainment industry."

LISTEN. HERE.

A close friend of mine: "One of my favorite things about you is that you can take what you dish out — narcissists suck at that. And entitled? If anything, I think you don't think that you deserve enough. And seeking attention? Girl, we can't even get you to have an Instagram account. I think you're good."

Now, y'all, I will be the first to yell with a bullhorn that we live in a culture that is *so arrogant* and *so insecure* (because, at the end of the day, they are pretty much different sides of the same coin; as I like to put it, arrogance is insecurity throwing a temper tantrum) that whenever you don't praise it or kiss its ass, somehow you are "shaming" or "judging" (we all need to be judged sometimes, by the way; that's what accountability is all about). Actually, the reality is that we need folks — folks who we can trust yet folks nonetheless — who are gonna tell us how they see us through their own eyes. Why? Because, if you only size yourself up based on your perception, your ego is definitely going to prevent you from noticing your character blind spots.

OK, so back to the kind narcissist and my second point. Remember how I said earlier in this book that when my mother and my brother's father were in the midst of raising me, they did have "A" moments? As far as my mother goes, one of them comes from when she used to say to me, "I just want you to be with a kind man." My late fiancé was that, for sure — and, over time, what I have learned is that you should always want a *kind* person over a *nice* one. That's why, although, again, I do appreciate the "kind narcissist" article that I read, also again, because being word-literal is totally my thing, I wish she would've gone with the word "nice" instead. Why? Well, while kind means benevolent, nice means agreeable, and when it comes to narcissistic people who are subtle and even covert (some might go so far as to say being sneaky too), usually they will play the role of being agreeable...because they have an agenda. Oh, but once they know that you have peeped their hustle, their stratagem, their game, it's then that all hell breaks loose. You see their temper. You see their vicious side. You see what people who only know them on a surface level (because they are really good at hiding the dark parts of their nature) never do. While everyone else is out here thinking that the nice narcissist is the epitome of humility and genuineness, it's a lie...in oh, so many ways, they are living a lie. And they are doing that because they are afraid to face the ugliness of who they truly are because it is easier to stay fake and receive praise than be real and receive true and lasting healing.

That said, I also want to put on record that although narcissists can be mean as hell (usually in waves), they aren't the devil; they are just severely broken. If you study the history of most of them, it's usually because their childhood was dysfunctional to the point where they had to come up with strange ways to protect themselves in order to survive — and that caused them to have a toxic relationship with their own ego. What life has taught me is that sometimes folks will try and take the narcissist on, kind of like a project. The challenge — no, problem — with that is, if you don't recognize them for the narcissist that they are before diving in — hell, if you're not completely sure that it's something you are called to do and not just something that you are calling yourself to experience — you will find yourself enduring abuse on levels you never really saw coming. I know this because I've done it before…and boy, do I have some bruises (especially on my knees from the prayers and fasting) to prove it.

And with that said, let's officially get into how and why this chapter has the title that it does.

Years ago, I was a house poet at a local (and pretty popular) spoken word joint here in Nashville. Another poet — who I couldn't be more different from and honestly penned and performed some pieces that were damn near terrifying at times — self-published a book that I purchased in support. I'll never forget how she opened it up: "The names have *not* been changed to convict the guilty." I know that I touched on this earlier, yet it really is wild how folks can treat you like their disposal diaper, glorified lap dog, doormat or simply their target for constant mental and emotional gaslighting, abuse, misuse and anguish, and yet, somehow, if their name is exposed for all the world to see, amazingly, the victim turns into the bad guy. SMDH. Yeah, another way to spot a narcissist is when they downplay the harm they caused while amplifying you calling them out on it.

That said, when I tell you that I kinda-sorta went back and forth with not withholding the guy who is the reason and purpose for this particular chapter, I was definitely see-sawing for a moment. The level of how much he has never really cared about the pain that he's caused me, even when I provided bullet point examples, along with the amount of time that he gaslit, deflected and almost seemed indignant about never apologizing for any of it — I honestly don't know how much mercy he actually deserves from me. And that's just the truth. Especially since, when I told ole' boy that he would be earning a chapter in this book due to all of his drama and trauma, whether he realized it or not, he actually cosigned on how truly diabolical he was by saying, "If I had known that you were going to write about it, I never would've…" and as his voice trailed off on the phone, I quickly jumped in and said, "What? Treated me like shit?", to which he replied with absolutely nothing but dead air. (Yeah, that's what I thought, negro.)

You know, I once read an article about signs that a man is truly manipulative. Some of them included that they are extremely charming; they like to play the victim; they always have a hidden agenda; they consistently use gaslighting as a tool; they enjoy exploiting your insecurities; they seek to downplay your strengths, and they don't know how to take accountability for their actions; instead, they deflect. Interesting. Very interesting. Anyway, I don't know why folks like to mess with writers. We literally document life for a living. It reminds me of a time when Jaguar Wright (who also has Seventh-Day Adventist ties and, if you know…you know) said in a random YouTube video that I once watched, "Look both ways before crossing my mind." LOL. So anyway, just a warning to others: If you involve yourself with writers — any kind of writer — and you don't want to read or hear about yourself in a not-so-awesome light someday, treat them/us better. It really is that simple. Sir, you once wrote about me. It was beautiful. Now I'm writing about you and it could've been different than this. Yet here is how you chose to be. Yep, here we are.

OK, so back to sharing his full government name. I really did have to check my motives (in this instance, making sure that I'm telling the story without trying to humiliate him for sport) because, there's no way that I can preach about accountability and not take a big heaping portion for myself. That would be called being a hypocrite, and I've seen more of that in my lifetime than I care to even admit. And so, since I'm not sure how comfortable I would be if I were in his shoes and my name was all out in the open, his shall be spared. I also plan to leave out the kind of details that will make it super obvious who I'm talking about (because, again…nosy folks, and for the billionth time, mercy). *He knows who he is.* I actually think he will only get this book to come to this chapter to see how "on blast" things are about to get. Well, Sir, I'm going to share *some* of what happened to me as it directly relates to you. Your identity isn't needed for that to be a cautionary tale for others when it comes to dealing with people who choose to move as you do. Yes, you dodged a bullet by my taking this approach in spite of all of the ones you shot my way (oh, and don't act like you didn't confirm that I never hurt you other than holding you accountable in a way that most never have; it's in an email. A lot of what you've done is documented in emails). You're welcome.

OK, so in order to extend the mercy that I just spoke of, I can't even really give the origin story of our journey. I'll just say that if there's one word to define our over 10-plus years (specific) walk, "serendipity" would have to be it. One example was God asking me to tell him something via an email, him not responding for days, my speaking at an event where a pastor backstage told me that I would be getting married and something special would happen that very day to confirm it; then my coming back to the place I was staying, only to receive a reply from said-guy. Another was attending an event where he was present, some friends of mine saying, "Shellie, we saw your husband. He was on the stage", my laughing at how often I had heard something similar regarding him, and then him saying those very people's names because they won a raffle at said-event. Another being, after almost a year of fasting for him until midnight for six-plus months and quite frankly being sick of his "come close, run away" routine in the midst of it all, a girlfriend at the time calling me to say that she had a dream that I brought him to her house, she held his face in her hands and spoke blessings over him, and that I should continue to "stand in the gap". Another is people saying to both of us that it seemed like we should be together because we physically resemble each other (and him even saying, "You probably will marry one of us. You look like my family."). Another is the countless times that we would run into each other and be completely matching in our outfits — odd colors, too, as we then stood in somebody's parking lot and talked for literal hours. Chile, the examples truly are endless.

Factoring all of this in, looking back, if I had to describe what we were, I'd probably simply say that what we had was a uniquely profound connection. "Uniquely profound" because I wouldn't exactly describe us as friends; friends treat each other better than he treated me. Uniquely profound because we never officially dated (even though he would say super arrogant and unself-aware stuff like, "I'm dating all of y'all. If I've taken you on a date, that's how I see it."). Uniquely profound because not one ounce of physical intimacy ever transpired past hugs, a hand-holding instance in a movie, and talks of sex — and if I were to be completely honest and accountable, the far-and-few between invites for copulation came from him while the intensely graphic talks about the act, in email form, believing that because there were so many serendipitous moments between us, surely one day we would share a marriage bed at some point, came from me. Uniquely profound because I can't tell you how many times this man was emotionally cruel and I kept taking it, thinking that it was something that I was "spiritually assigned" to do.

Why would I put it on God? That's a fair question. It's because, when I first met this man (via a friend of his who also...very emotionally complicated), I wasn't interested in him in the way that so many others seemed to be. I actually found him to be quite cute and very corny. However, when I felt that God instructed me to take him on as a spiritual task, all of the praying, fasting and connecting in that way, it caused me to believe that we were ultimately destined to be together; that all of those wildly happenstance moments were a universal cosign to something that he actually said to me at the beginning of our journey: "I promise to strive to get into position for this life and for us. You are wonderful." (Yeah, that's in an email too, my guy. You really should deal with this as it comes.)

You know, it can be dangerous having your primary love language be words of affirmation. Looking back, I know that is exactly why I let so much of his nonsense slide; it's because my love language will cause me to take people at their word instead of requiring actions to back it all up. In hindsight, that one reply caused me to overlook so much mental and emotional agony because, I believed that he was simply broken and immature; therefore, if I was to serve as his Nehemiah and stand in the gap like my friend said (Nehemiah 1) or his Anaias and offer support until "Saul" transformed into "Paul" (Acts 9)…so be it.

OK, so why do I say that he was an emotionally cruel type of individual? It's because I know what the word means: "willfully or knowingly causing pain or distress to others". And how do I know, without question, that he was that way towards me? Oh, I've got some examples for that too. And these are only a few of 'em.

I mean, there was the time when one of his concubines (that's what I call women who are sexually active with men while there not being much else within their dynamic), who was married, called him to tell him that she didn't like seeing us out together and him then emailing me talking about he didn't like that I made his friends uncomfortable (dude…*she's married*. What are you even talking about?).

Him starting arguments on my birthday and then saying things like, "You might have a happy birthday but it's not gonna be because of me." (Umm, so you like ruining special days?)

Speaking of birthdays, him once sending me an email at the beginning of one of mine — the day everyone who knows me knows matters most — at midnight to say that he thought I aged beautifully *and* that he wanted me to know that he was seeing someone. *So, you decide to start off my birthday by telling me you're dating someone else?* And when I brought up to him how tacky, at the very least, that was, his flippant response was, "I say things when they come to mind in order to get them off my chest, even if it's a special day." (You really are something else.)

Him lying about his relationship with one of his concubines, leaving me in the parking lot with her, her giving me all of the dirty details because she was also a supreme gaslighter and then him yelling at me on the phone the next day for listening to her talk to me about them — even though he knew that I had feelings for him and even though he was the one who sped out of the parking lot like a true coward.

Him having me put on an event for him, one that I produced from start to finish, *for free*, my asking him to stay on the phone with me to keep me awake as we both were driving over an hour back home in separate cars in the middle of the night after it was over, only for him to yell at me again (yes, literally) for even asking for his help in the first place. Remember, I did all of the work...FOR FREE.

My working for him for over two years and, quite frankly, getting him more solid media traction than I've seen on him to-date and receiving $200, twice, over that period of time. (Do you remember that I have your social security number? You are both bold and clueless as hell.)

Him being hella cryptic about a woman he was seeing, me point-blank asking him if they were dating and him replying, "I might be her boyfriend but she's definitely not my girlfriend." (Bless her heart.)

Us having a four-hour-plus conversation, while he was on a road trip, about our relationship, him saying that he was trying to choose between two different paths (me and the nongirlfriend-girlfriend I just spoke of), the cell signal dropping, my thinking that it was one of our best conversations ever, only to get another one of his damn emails in the middle of the night that said a bunch of nonsense along with, "I will never marry you. EVER." Then dodging calls from me as I tried to figure out just what the hell was going on — FOR THE BILLIONTH TIME.

Him, months later, asking me to attend an event because there was something that he wanted to tell me, him making an announcement about his engagement and then claiming that he "forgot" what he wanted me to come for in the first place (again, how diabolical ARE you?).

See what I mean? *Supreme gaslighting.*

See what I mean? *Profound cruelty.*

And just in case you're not exactly sure what gaslighting is, it's when someone gets off on manipulating you *so much* that it's basically at the point where you wonder if what you know to be real *is* real. *That was him.* Whenever I did something wrong or even that he simply didn't like (which isn't the same thing as wrong, by the way), he would either try and guilt trip me or berate me to death. On the other hand, whenever I would call him out on his mess, he would simply shift responsibility or throw some flippant line out like, "Well, hurt people, hurt people." No, dear. What you have are issues. You need to do better. *You need to do the inner work to get better.*

The Bible says that charm is deceitful (Proverbs 31:30) and boy, did this guy ever drive that point home. Yet, in hindsight, who I think he deceives more than anyone is himself. Now, for the record, I don't think that he's Satan's son's best friend, I really don't. I just think that he is a hustling narcissist who lacks very little personal accountability and people like that can justify, pretty much whatever they do. In fact, he once told me that one of the things that bothered him so much about me is the fact that his two closest friends never "stress him out" because they don't call him out like I do. My immediate reply to that was simply, "So, how are they your friends if they never tell you when you're wrong?" Those kinds of people are *fans* not *friends*. And you know what? Narcissists tend to like it that way.

What's really wild is, because he is so caught up in thinking that fandom is friendship, to this day, he doesn't realize just how many Judases are at his life's table. Women who smile in his face while joking about what it was like to be with him (in every room of the house) behind his back as they say taunting things about his current relationship. Guys who look for ways to make opportunities happen by being in his space as they stand grinning in pictures along his side. It's truly amazing to behold because, while he actually believes that he's got everyone fooled, he's being fooled — by his own reflection. Egos don't tell us the truth; egos flatter and the Bible frowns on flattery because flattery always has a selfish motive. Yeah, flattery cannot be trusted: *"He who speaks flattery to his friends, even the eyes of his children will fail."* (Job 17:5 — NKJV)

...

So, with all of this said, do I have a conclusion for what my journey with him was all about? That is such a marvelous question. Also, since he was so low-down, on so many levels, do I still believe that he was a spiritual assignment? Funny enough, I do — an assignment, a lesson, and a revelation...on a few levels.

I'm not sure that I ever would've connected the dots about narcissism on the level that I now have had I not experienced him. After I finally got sick of nursing my wounds from his blows, I started really looking into narcissism and narcissistic abuse — a very telling sign that you are being abused by a narcissist is if you're constantly putting your own needs aside in order to make or keep them happy (some others include defending the abuser and walking on eggshells just to keep the peace, which includes apologizing to the narcissist for things that they did wrong, just so they won't stay mad at you).

I've learned that some relationship-based sayings are a complete sham. One, for example, is "If you want to watch how a man is going to treat you, watch how he treats his mother." Chile, please let that lie go. Right now, I can easily name 15 guys who have shared enough of their dynamic with their mother while growing up that lets me know that they "treat her like a queen" — *out of fear*. Fear of what? Fear of having some real conversations about how much she dropped the ball while raising them. Some guys, because they also didn't have the best dad experiences, they will turn their mom into a mini-god because they will damn near have a nervous breakdown if they are honest with themselves about how flawed she truly was and/or is. And so, instead of having some hard talks with her, they treat the women they date like crap. They project their anger and disgust onto us. This guy is one of the 15, for sure, because there ain't no way that you can love your mama the way that you claim and be as cruel to women as you are — or at least used to be. In fact, one time, while we were having a conversation about some of the women who he's dated in the past and how he's treated them, I said, "I don't think you like women very much", to which he simply shrugged his shoulders and said, "I don't." Yeah, don't just go by how a man treats his mother. *Dig into that childhood shit*. Sometimes the "pampering" is performative — whether the guy knows (or accepts) it or…not.

FREE. WILL. If there is one thing that always trips me out about humanity, it's the fact that everyone likes free will when it comes to the choices that *they* make — oh, but then they want God to use all kinds of force if others aren't doing what *they* want. Yeah, that's not how it works. That's why, whenever folks will say something like, "If

God is such a good God, why did that great person get killed by that drunk driver?", I kind of roll my eyes. Y'all, that wasn't because of God, that was because someone was driving drunk; that was their free will operating irresponsibly. And because God doesn't renege on what he sets into motion like humans do, he has to respect everyone's right to choose. That said, do I believe that God wanted me to stand in the gap for this guy, in spite of how things ultimately turned out? I do. Do I think that, just the physical sexual purity between us alone (something that I think has been a very rare experience for him), made our connection extraordinary? I do. Do I also think that sometimes the Most High can show us something (or someone) magnificent, and, based on where we are spiritually and personally at the time, we may choose them — or not? Yes. Y'all, we've got to stop thinking that God wasn't real when he came to us about certain persons, places, things and/or ideas if they don't ultimately manifest. Free will has to be factored in at all times.

Reaping what you sow. I don't know too many Scriptures in the Bible that are more sobering than Galatians 6:7-8; especially since it never tells us how long the reaping will last. OK, so did I "deserve" to be treated with so much disdain? No. "Deserve" isn't the right word (especially since this guy professes to be a believer); however, have I been flippant with people's feelings before? Yep. Have I taken someone's care for me completely for granted more than once? Sure have. Have I projected some of my own issues onto someone else, simply because they let me? Yep. Listen, be careful what you sow out in these streets. I can't tell you how many times I have sat across from a married person (who claims to be a believer) who is ready to leave their union because their spouse cheated and then when I say, "So, did y'all have sex before you got married?" and they say "yes", I simply say, "Well, now you know how God feels." Wild how we're OK with breaking his (biblical) boundaries, and yet, we have no mercy or grace for when someone disregards our own. There goes that ego thing again. SOWING. WILL. REAP. PLEASE. SOW. WISELY.

Don't let someone get you out of character. Another reason why I think that this guy definitely needed extensive therapy (and I hope he eventually gets it) is because he seemed to take pleasure in "leveling women out" — usually sexually. What I mean by that is, if he was able to conquer you on the sex tip, it gave him an odd sense of pride and power over you (if that doesn't sound truly narcissistic and toxic, what does?). And again, that is something that he will NEVER get to say about me because, as sexual as a person that I am, I knew not to give him any of ANYTHING (Matthew 7:6) unless we were husband and wife; he would be unsafe otherwise (due to all of what I just said). And because he could never "put me in my place" in that fashion and honestly, because he never got me to straight up snap on him in some ways that my tribe is still awed that I haven't done, I think sometimes he would "turn up the dial" on the meanness, just to get me to become someone different than who I professed to be. Why? It's because, if I got out of myself, he could rationalize his actions and justify them too. Listen, I used to wonder why some women would take extreme measures on him (I'll leave those details out because, again, nosy people). I DO NOW. And no, he doesn't deserve for me to give him so much power that I lose who I am. *Never give someone so much power that you lose yourself.*

Anything that strengthens your spiritual life serves a profound purpose. Personally, I'm not a fan of the saying, "Everything happens for a reason." I mean, *duh.* Nah, you'd be far better off with "things happen for a purpose" — things happening so that you can become more solidified in your own purpose. And I must say that my experience with this individual strengthened my prayer and fasting life, taught me how to not "match energy" all of the time, helped me to see how God feels oftentimes when he is good and consistent with us and we just keep on showing out anyway — and how to handle people who have extreme qualities and issues — because even with all of what I just said, there are some things about this person that are very good. I can only imagine how much better they would've been had he not been so, Lord, wounded. Anyway, although a lot of what he did to me was bad, how I chose to respond to it was good — and that has strengthened me for the next leg of life's journey. All things work together. And what about the couple in the mall who said that he was my soulmate and he was refusing to grow up? Yeah, I've spent a lot of time studying that word too; it's not a Disney term. Bashert, which is usually reserved for a marital dynamic, is one type of soulmate while other soulmate is someone who literally strengthens your soul in a way that no one else can due to the uncanny connection that you have with them. That said, one way or another, they didn't lie.

Learn the lesson. So that you don't repeat it. I say it often, because I believe it to be so: God is the kind of teacher who doesn't let you "skip a grade" in life just because you've chosen to not learn the lesson over and over...and over again. I don't want to hurt people like that man has hurt me. Lesson learned. I can spot a narcissist a mile away now — pretty much in all forms. Lesson learned. I really do like the fact that I am the same way no matter who I'm around; that I'm not a chameleon. Chameleons can't trust anyone, not even themselves; they switch up too much. When you see those, they are cautionary tales. Lesson learned. Even if a man is vacillating about you, even if he says that he doesn't want you out of fear or anger, let him lose you. As I've said in other chapters, be OK with being someone's consequence; sometimes they aren't going to learn any other way. Lesson learned. Being a believer and actually being spiritually mature are not even close to being the same things. Lesson learned. People who lack self-awareness are dangerous. Lesson learned. If you feel used, you are being used. Lesson learned. People tend to love others based on their understanding and experience of love, not the biblical or healthy standard; so, before you run with someone saying that they love you (however, they opt to express it — and you know what I mean by that, Sir), qualify it. I Corinthians 13 is an awesome place to start. Lesson learned. You can't build anything truly lasting with someone who loathes accountability. Lesson learned. Some folks don't want a true partner; they simply want an audience. Lesson learned. If someone doesn't choose you, God is bigger than the rejection. Rest in that. Lesson learned.

And from the lessons, what is the revelation? I now realize that, because so much of my life consisted of dealing with wounded people, I was used to being damn near supernaturally resilient when it came to tolerating abuse — I thought that was what love required. Now? Eh, not so much. As I was just telling a client recently, we must always remember that sacrifice means that we are giving up something good for something greater. And so, whenever you find yourself in a position where that is not happening, you are not sacrificing, you are participating in a twisted form of self-harm — and oftentimes it's because you were never really given the skills to self-protect (well) in the first place. And so, by experiencing this journey with the nice guy narcissist, ironically, I've learned how to not settle for nice, even within myself--to not "be in agreement" at the expense of being truly kind to me. When you're a survivor of abuse, you don't know what kindness really looks like. When you're healed from abuse, you require it — of everyone and everything around you.

Hmph. Y'all see how long this chapter is, right? There is a bit more ground to cover, and so, I've got to bring all of this to a close. And while

I won't exactly say "thank you" to the nice guy narcissist, what I will say is, "You tried to break me and you didn't." I love that. For both of us. It has strengthened me. It has humbled your ego (whether your ego has allowed you to realize it yet or not). I now get that I took so much from you because "taking it" was the norm to me. Narcissistic abuse was the norm for me.

However, instead of becoming one of y'all, I graduated from the lessons and embraced the revelation. By not letting your toxicity (and honestly, your own pain) infect me to the point of altering me — like so many others before you always tried to do — I am fully free.

Serving you, *freed me*. I am now truly kind to myself. Now, more than ever, I require kindness of others.

Now isn't that — pardon the pun here. LOL. — NICE? Indeed, dear sir. Indeed, it is.

(By the way, the folks who had a front seat to all of this wanted me to let you know that they think you got off hella easy — that you received *way more mercy* than you actually deserve. Some of those people are in your face fairly regularly too. Hmph. Again, you're welcome.)

"So, Jesus said to those Jews who had
believed in Him, 'If you abide in My word hold
fast to My teachings and live in accordance
with them, you are truly My disciples.
And you will know the Truth, and the Truth
will set you free.'"

(JOHN 8:31-32-AMPC)

Chapter Nine

I Am Not a Christian. There Is So Much Freedom in Saying That.

Something that I hear often — from church folks, that is — is how surprised people are by how much Word that I know; sometimes stuff that many of them don't even know themselves. Take something fascinating that I discovered via the Message Version of the Bible many years ago. OK, so you know when that New Age book *The Secret* came out and everyone was going crazy over it? Personally, I find it interesting how much culture likes to repackage something that Scripture has already addressed while acting like they came up with the concept. Oh, but that's the ego for you.

What do I mean in this case? I mean, *The Secret* is basically all about the law of attraction, right? At the end of the day, isn't *"For as he thinks in his heart, so is he"* (Proverbs 23:7 — NKJV) pretty much the same thing? Anyway, because I know and associate with people from all walks of life, I had all kinds of folks who wanted me to check the book out. From day one, I was good on that. I didn't need a reason; my spirit didn't sit well with it...simple as that. Then one day, I did receive a confirmation about why I felt that way. It was a pretty wild one at that:

"I want you woven into a tapestry of love, in touch with every-thing there is to know of God. Then you will have minds confident and at rest, focused on Christ, God's great mystery. All the richest treasures of wisdom and knowledge are embedded in that mystery and nowhere else. ___And we've been shown the mystery! I'm telling you this because I don't want anyone leading you off on some wild-goose chase, after other so-called mysteries, or 'the Secret'.___*"* (Colossians 2:2-4 — Message)

Now watch this. The Message Version of Scripture? It was first published in 1993. The book *The Secret*? It was first published in 2006. Y'all can debate amongst yourselves if that is just a random occurrence or not. For me, it's just one example of how I am thankful that I listen, spiritually, differently. It has spared me a lot, caused me to thrive in my purpose in ways I never would've otherwise, and it has caused me to come to some very unique, satisfying and inner peace conclusions.

THAT SAID...

Is the title for this chapter clickbait? Eh, maybe a little bit; that doesn't make it any less true, though. As you already read in a previous chapter, yes, I was raised Adventist and yes, that is a denomination within the Christian faith. That said, honestly, I've been trying to get my name off of the Adventist membership ledger for years now (how y'all gonna *make* someone stay on? Even God himself gives us free will) because there is very little that the denomination and I have in common at this point. Also, I've already shared just how word-literal I am, ad nauseum, which is why I am also good on the Christian title too. Yeah, because I tend to do a lot of digging and research on, just about any and everything, I know the origin story of the word "Christian". To say that I am not a fan? That doesn't even begin to scratch the surface of how I feel about the word (and a lot of the people who claim to be one — and yet, I digress).

Some scholars say that "Christian" comes from the Greek word *"christianos,"* which means "little Christs". Chile, even *that* creeps me out because, I'm with the late and great Maya Angelou, who once said (I heard her say it myself at a venue here in Nashville), "How do y'all just walk around saying that 'I'm Christlike'? I'm in my 80s and don't think that." Indeed. Adding to that, I also know that, back in the biblical times, when Christ's disciples believed that he had risen from the dead, unbelievers called his followers "Christians" as a way of mocking them. Yes, *"Christian" was a mockery word* — and from the way a lot of these folks out here who profess to be Christians act, both in and out of the church? On so many levels, that still seems to remain quite true. I mean, mock doesn't just mean "to attack or treat with ridicule, contempt, or derision"; mock also means "to mimic, imitate or counterfeit". Hmph. I just "threw" it. Either you caught it by reading between the lines or…you didn't. #Elmoshrug

Besides, Christ never said that his followers were "his Christians". The Bible that I read says that he told us that if we know the truth and desire the freedom that comes along with it (kind of like how making confessions known instead of sneaking, hiding, ducking 'n dodging would heal us — James 5:16), we were his DISCIPLES (John 8:31-32). Disciples? Yeah, that sounds so much better than thinking that we are little Christs when we absolutely are not. Yes, we should strive to be more and more like Christ; however, that desire doesn't automatically make the outcome so. Let me tell it, there's a ton of arrogance that comes in thinking otherwise…which is why spiritual narcissism running rampant in so many of these churches makes all of the sense in the world.

Meanwhile, being a disciple comes with things like being self-disciplined (instead of merely emotionalizing our way in and out of things, gaslighting ourselves and others by having a selective memory, and/or throwing some random Scripture at a matter and then acting like it's *Showtime at the Apollo*, meaning you shouldn't be challenged, just because you played a verse like Joker card in a game of Spades). It reminds you that disciples are followers more than anything else. For me personally, it also reminds me that, contrary to the faith that I grew up in or the bold presumption that so many denominations have (there being hundreds of ways to come to the Lord is straight-up ridiculous, by the way), no, I do not have all of the truth. Disciples will never reach the totality of truth while living on this earth. We are students and (hopefully) then scholars until we die and prayerfully make it to heaven (yeah, while we're on this topic, that's something else that is annoying about Christians; just like you don't know if someone is going to hell, you don't know if they are going to heaven either. *God is the final judge — both ways.* Funerals need to be conducted with way more spiritual responsibility and accuracy instead of being so emotionally-driven — Ecclesiastes 3:17).

So, no, for these reasons and more, I am not a Christian. And boy, am I thrilled about that; especially since I know that I wouldn't have come into the knowledge of so many things that I have learned since leaving all of that behind me.

Things like what? Honestly, I'm learning something new and/or spiritually inspiring on an almost daily basis, so it's impossible to share everything. What I will break down are some things about my name, my birthday and how immersing myself in Hebrew culture has totally changed my life for the better (my purpose plays a role in all of this too; I will address that in the final chapter of this book).

Name first. So, according to my mother, I was going to have a unisex name: Ryan. It means "little leader". Yet she said that once

I was born, "You came out and looked like a little Indian, so I called you, 'Shellie'. I felt like the Holy Spirit told me to." For years, I did my best to just accept that, although it never made much sense to me. I mean, I saw those corny refrigerator magnets with the name meanings on them and my name always said something along the lines of "peaceful meadow" — yeah, something just didn't "jive" with me on that. Then, one day, when I was in my late 30s, I was walking around in my favorite mall and an Israeli woman at a skincare kiosk said in her strong accent, "You're pretty. What's your name?" I don't know what made me decide to entertain that sales pitch on that particular day — well, I guess I *do* know: It had to be the Holy Spirit (John 4:24 — AMPC). Clearly, it was time for me to hear why he said what he did to my mother all those years before.

When I responded with, "Uh-huh, I don't want any of your products," she said, "No, I really do think you're pretty. What's your name?" as she looked at me with firm intention.

When I said, "Shellie", she immediately said, "Ah, you have a Hebrew name." When I looked at her like she was crazy, she then said, "It's very common at home. It means 'Mine; Belonging to Me.' It means that you belong to God."

Not that I thought Lital (that was her name) was lying or anything; however, after she said that, I was so caught off guard that I immediately looked it up — and yep, she knew exactly what she was talking about. The Hebrew word for mine is "sheli" and the context is oftentimes in reference to Adonai. Wow. Then, when I got home and prayed for a Scriptural reference, Ezekiel 16 is what I was led to. A part of it says, *"'When I passed by you again and looked upon you, indeed your time was the time of love; so, I spread My wing over you and covered your nakedness. Yes, I swore an oath to you and entered into a covenant with you, and you became Mine,' says the Lord God."* (Ezekiel 16:8 — NKJV)

Covenant. Whenever people ask me what my purpose is, I simply say that it is marriage, sex and the (true) Sabbath (which isn't Sunday; if we all agree that Christ died on Good Friday and rose on Sunday, Matthew 28:1 says that Sunday is the first day of the week. If Christ respected the Sabbath enough to remain dead on it, how much more should followers of him honor it? It's not rocket science...folks just don't like to keep covenant; covenant-keeping is not for the weak). The thing these three points have in common is covenant. There's a chapter that I have that's devoted to that, so let's move on to another thing that I find to be fascinating.

My birthday. Actually, before running into Lital, I discovered something wild about the day that I was born. Now, my family, we run Gemini deep. My mother is a Gemini. Her husband is a Gemini. My brother is a Gemini. Both of my paternal grandparents are Geminis. My mom's brother is a Gemini. And although I don't treat *astrology* like a religion, I am aware that on the fourth day of creation (Genesis 1:14-19), stars were used as a sign, and so there is a science in *astronomy* (some of y'all really need to relax; saying that "5" means grace or "8" means "new beginnings" is a form of numerology, and you church folks say stuff like that on the regular). That said, several years back, there were some scientists who said they believe that they know when Christ's actual birthday is because it's not the lie that it is December 25. The origin story of the paganism of that holiday is Christians wanted to be a part of the winter solstice festival (Google all of the foolishness that used to go down on that day, chile) *so badly* that they tacked Christ's birthday onto the end of it to justify participating in it. To this day, Christians all over the world will say things like, "We know it's not his actual birthday but..." *How silly do they sound?* Do you want someone not observing *your* real birthday? *Exactly.* Anyway, back to my main point. Scientists believe that Christ's birthday is June 17. My birthday? Yep, you guessed it: June 17. Two days after my mother was born. In 1974, it happened to be that I was born an hour after Father's Day (pretty sure that's a part of the reason why I go so hard for my father even now; very few ever spoke up for him). In Jewish culture, Sivan falls in May or June (depending on the year). That is when they honor Moses receiving the Torah (the Law). Tammuz can fall in June or July (again depending on the year); it is tied to things like worship, vision and covenant. COVENANT. My name means covenant. I was born in the season of covenant. Well, looka there. #wink

And then there's me and Hebrew culture. People close to me have heard me say, shoot, at least two dozen times in some sort of conversation that I find it to be hypocritically comical that folks will claim to be followers of Christ — Christ, the King of the Jews (Matthew 27:11), no less — and yet won't eat like him, won't observe the holy days that he did, won't honor the Sabbath (the one that he stayed in a state of spiritual rest on; it can't be said enough). Umm, how is Christ "your best friend" when you don't even have a lot in common with the man? Since he was a Jew, why do so many Christians know so little about Judaism and/or refuse to put so much about it into practice? It's très bizarre. Very much so. And since it seems like only a handful of Christians (you know, in the grand scheme of things) even have a clue about Hebrew culture, that's another reason why it would be a lie for me to call myself one.

Examples: If you are a Christian who is reading this, did you know that, according to Hebrew studies, Proverbs 31 is actually the eulogy that Abraham wrote for Sarah? Or that Boaz died on his wedding night? Or that Orpah is Goliath's mother? Since there is no "J" in the Hebrew alphabet, why do the "little Christs" not actually call Christ by his true name: Yehoshua? Because, before Greek, there was Hebrew (yes, I know that Jesus is tied to Joshua and that it is somewhat of a long story; doesn't change the point that I'm making, though). The denomination that I grew up in that boasts of having all of the "truth", I didn't learn this from them; these are things that I didn't learn until I became *intentional* about learning Hebrew culture. Had I pompously and delusionally thought that the denomination that I grew up in had all of the "truth" that I needed to know, I doubt that these other truths would've ever come my way — and that would've hindered my spiritual and purpose-related growth. Know what else it would've done? It would've stagnated the expansion of my purpose too because, if you get nothing else out of this chapter, please hear me when I say that, when you are fully engrossed in living out your purpose, it just keeps getting bigger and bigger....AND BIGGER.

...

So, since my name means covenant and I was born in the season of covenant, it would actually make all of the sense in the world that my life's work would be surrounded around covenant principles — ones that, quite frankly, Christians, overall, are pretty poor at honoring: marriage, sex and the true Sabbath. I liken it to the Israelites who wandered around in the wilderness for 40 years vs. the ones who actually made it into the Promised Land — all loved God on some level; few really walked in true agreement with him, though. Covenant requires true agreement not just convenient service.

And yes, that has made my life journey remarkable, even to me. When I'm not writing about marriage, sex and/or the Sabbath, I am working with couples (especially ones who seek to reconcile their divorce, which are those who *really get* the magnitude of their marital covenant). In between that, over the past 20 years, I have mentored teen mothers; worked for years with an organization that gets people out of porn and sex addiction; written another book (that was a part of a trilogy for that organization); spoken at colleges and other events all over the country, and no matter what, what it has all come back to, somehow, some way, is covenant-keeping — and you know what? *Covenant-keeping is a core value of discipleship.* I dare say, this is not really the case when it comes to Christianity because, all I hear (the majority of American) Christians discuss is how they can justify and excuse their way out of honoring what the Word actually says about marriage, or the value of sex (especially in marriage — shoot, with I Corinthians 7:5 alone), or why now, we are not under a "new law" that says it's OK not to keep the Seventh-Day Sabbath. Hmph. Funny how y'all are good with still tithing when that isn't in the New Testament at all (Malachi 3), and yet you can't be bothered with the actual Sabbath Christ honored and is mentioned multiple times in the New Testament. Make it make sense (you can't, so don't even try). Plus, Google the history of Constantine sometime. Then research the influence of Catholicism on your religion. It will do you some good. Shoot, even the amount of people who have no clue that "trinity" is not a biblical word (Godhead refers to God, Christ and the Holy Spirit — I John 5:8) is a plum trip.

Christianity will have you thinking stuff like this doesn't matter; it'll also have you confusing the difference between grace and mercy too. *Discipleship*, though? It doesn't waver. It doesn't "change with the times" (or culture). It doesn't put what's popular before what is actually true and right (Luke 6:26 — Message).

Now, is discipleship perfection? Absolutely not. I mean, have you researched the lives of Christ's disciples (I personally know with everything in me that Peter and I are related — LOL)? However, are they cookie cutter? Nope. Are they willing to make great sacrifices? Yep. Will they totally go against the grain, no matter what? Absolutely. There are very few Christians (who I know) who I can say that about. The few who choose to forego that title and go with "disciple" instead? They all fit the bill.

You know, something that I am is a professional certified life coach. A big part of what that means is knowing how to ask the right questions that will lead people to some "ah-ha moments" for themselves. That said, there is a Canadian theologian by the name of John B. MacDonald who once said, "Asking questions and encouraging questions are powerful tools for making disciples." Hmph. Think about all of the churches that are getting away from Sabbath or Sunday school. I won't get into how many church forums I've been to where leaders will cut off mics whenever someone makes a point that challenges them or they don't like (the egos of church leaders have gotten so out of hand!). If you've never read *Pagan Christianity: Exploring the Roots of Our Church Practices* (Viola/Barna) before, check it out sometime; this notion that you should pack into a building to hear only one person speak while cheering like it's a concert featuring your favorite artist? Pagan. Christianity would never bring me to all of this because it literally bucks against their agenda. Discipleship has, though.

So yeah, if while reading this book, you were somewhere in your mind like, "This girl is nowhere near being a Christian" — to that I would first say, "thank you" and then I would follow it up with, "you are absolutely right". I've never done what is popular. I've never fit in. And I am more than OK with that. I am elated and quite clear that being this way has brought me peace and made me whole.

And no, you do not have to understand it. All of the true disciples out here? They do, though.

Ask them.

*"There's trouble ahead when
you live only for the approval of others,
saying what flatters them, doing what indulges them.
Popularity contests are not truth contests—
look how many scoundrel preachers were
approved by your ancestors! Your task is
to be true, not popular."*

(LUKE 6:26-MESSAGE)

Chapter Ten

Marriage. Sex.
The Sabbath.

Whenever I speak publicly on dating, courtship, engagement and marriage, one thing that I will say, easily 95 percent of the time, is I don't fall for that "men are hunters" crap. So many people say stuff, on repeat, for so long, that they don't even stop to think if it's healthy, wise or if it even makes any real sense or not. From a biblical perspective, why in the world does a man need to "hunt" a gift from the Lord (James 1:17) and why would a woman want to be "hunted" like prey? Have mercy. *The foolishness.* Please, let's make it stop, especially if you profess to be a believer, because again, the only time perfection is in the Bible is the Garden of Eden and Adam was not a *hunter*; Adam was a *gardener*. If you read Genesis 2:18-25, Adam didn't do ANYTHING when it came to receiving his wife, the Woman (again, "Eve" was her name post-sin — Genesis 3:20); that man was asleep (unconscious) as she was being prepared for him. Adding to that, what Scripture says is that GOD BROUGHT HER TO HIM (which is probably where fathers walking their daughters down the aisle originated — Genesis 2:22). I discern that God did it that way, so that both Adam and his *ezer kenegdo* (which is Hebrew for helpmate; it loosely translates into the word "lifesaver") would know that, when it comes to a God-ordained dynamic, we need to let the Creator do most of the work. I mean, have y'all seen the divorce stats lately? For those of you who are also caught up in the notion that only men should make the first move (so, some of y'all think that submission is obsolete, yet you want men to make the first move? Conflicted much? Also, some of you need to re-read how Ruth and Esther got down — they pursued, for sure), most men don't know how to pick well; they truly need to *fully submit* to God's selection process. Both genders do. And then move accordingly.

And what does all of this have to do with the title of this chapter? Well, a part of the reason why I am able to see things from this perspective is due to my purpose. You know, so many people — so many people who are considered to be successful as far as how our culture defines success to be — have no idea what their purpose is; that's unfortunate too because it is literally the reason why each of us exist; we are each here to serve a clear and specific end...aim...goal. And so, because I am very aware of mine, whenever people ask me to give them a "purpose hack", what I tend to say is, "If you can't explain your purpose in three words or phrases, there's a pretty good chance that you don't know exactly what it is." My reasoning behind this is because, when you know why you're here, explaining it shouldn't be complicated. Not only that but because I know that trinity literally means "three in one", another reason why I think that "three" is the go-to number for purpose is because the reason why you are here should be ingrained in every part of you: your mind, your body and your spirit. All of them should work together to make manifesting your purpose easier to do.

That said, as for myself, my purpose is marriage, sex and the Sabbath — not the versions of these that have been manipulated by both the world *and* the Church. I mean, these three things in the way that the Word presents them — no editing, no figuring out a way to make it fit what we want, no tweaking it to suit how Westernized culture and society does things. And so, what does that entail? This, too, is its own book. I will do my best to scratch the surface in one chapter, though.

Back when I was working with an organization that got people out of porn and sex addiction, a woman named Michelle who worked there said something to me that actually kind of pissed me off in the moment; now, I get that she just may be onto something: "Shellie, I'm not sure if you're ever going to get married. One, you know a lot about marriage in a way that most people don't and two, I'm starting to think that you *are* 'Christ's bride'...literally." She even purchased a book about it for me. At the time, my thinking was that because I was called to learn and teach about marital covenant (which is apart from how most humans tend to "do marriage", which is honestly a mockery of covenant) that surely, I would end up with a husband of my very own. Hmph — maybe, maybe not. That's the thing about purposes (Proverbs 16:4 — AMPC) and callings (Romans 11:29): sometimes they come with the sacrifice of not getting all of what you desire in life (Hebrews 11). On this side of living, I've made peace with that: *"Many plans are in a man's mind, but it is the Lord's purpose for him that will stand."* (Proverbs 19:21 — AMPC)

OK, so back to what I know that I am called to do, as far as marriage is concerned. First, I'm to remind people that marriage is not "just a relationship"; *it's supposed to be a covenant*. That is a high honor and it's also something that comes with a lot — and I do mean, A LOT — of responsibility. In fact, if you look at Scripture, only one relational dynamic even comes close to the Godhead. Peep it:

*"And there are three that bear witness on earth: the Spirit, the water, and the blood; **and these three agree as one**."* (I John 5:8 — AMPC)

*"Therefore, a man shall leave his father and mother and be joined to his wife, **and they shall become one flesh**. And they were both naked, the man and his wife, and were not ashamed"* (Genesis 2:24-25 — NKJV)

Oneness means things like "sameness" and "unity of thought, feeling, belief, aim, etc.; agreement; concord" and since covenant literally means "agreement", that literally tracks. And although I do work with singles, engaged and married couples, my "niche" is reconciling divorces. Why? Because, contrary to how our church culture teaches — and, quite frankly, mocks — marriage, divorce was never God's plan. Know what else? Neither was marrying someone else while your original spouse is still alive. Christ made it clear that MOSES <u>not</u> GOD came up with divorce (Matthew 19:1-12), that God HATES divorce (Malachi 2:14-16), and that if people do get divorced, this is now they are to handle it: *"Now to the married I command, yet not I but the Lord: A wife is not to depart from her husband. But even if she does depart, let her remain unmarried or be reconciled to her husband. And a husband is not to divorce his wife"* (I Corinthians 7:10-11 — NKJV) Oh, but because Westernized Christians like to romanticize, emotionalize and, quite frankly, twist and turn the Bible to make it "submit" to them, Christians actually have the highest divorce rate of any faith in this country (including agnostic and atheist people). That should be embarrassing as literal hell, especially since one of the main things that Christians like to quote is that husbands should love their wives as Christ loved the Church — uh-huh...*when did Christ divorce the Church*? And y'all, church folks of his time (known as Pharisees) plotted to kill that man (Matthew 12:14)!

So, how did divorce get so out of control? Well, that's where applying culture to Scripture comes in. Back in Moses's day, folks took both marriage and sex far more seriously than they do now (honestly, that is probably the greatest understatement in this book). Not only that but, back then, divorce actually had to do with if a man was betrothed (which is basically engaged) to a woman, he found out that she lied about her virginity and he wanted to rescind his offer of intent to marry her because of it — because, back then, when you said that you would do something, you did it. Your word was literally your bond. Your word had integrity attached to it. You didn't abuse words like "mercy" and "grace" to justify breaking your word. And how do I know all of this? Because Joseph, Christ's earthly father, considered divorcing Mary, remember? And no, they were not married yet:

"Now the birth of Jesus Christ took place under these circumstances: When His mother Mary had been promised in marriage to Joseph, **_before they came together_**_, she was found to be pregnant [through the power] of the Holy Spirit. And her [promised] husband Joseph, being a just and upright man and not willing to expose her publicly and to shame and disgrace her,_ **_decided to repudiate and dismiss (divorce) her quietly and secretly_**_. But as he was thinking this over, behold, an angel of the Lord appeared to him in a dream, saying, 'Joseph, descendant of David, do not be afraid to take Mary [as] your wife, for that which is conceived in her is of (from, out of) the Holy Spirit.'"* (Matthew 1:18-20 — AMPC)

Back then, it wasn't common to have sex before marriage. Back then, a part of a woman's virtue was her virginity. Back then, there were grave consequences that came from getting married without purity being in place. All of that is another talk for another time. For now, I just want you to get that Joseph wasn't married and yet he was considering divorcing Mary. THIS is why Moses — again, MOSES not GOD — came up with divorce. *THIS is also why adultery is not infidelity; it is marrying a divorced person* — again, Scripture makes that abundantly clear. How folks keep trying to overlook all of this never ceases to amaze me.

And honestly, it's no wonder that Christians divorce the most of any other religion over here, will boldly marry other people, pretty much like it's nothing, and then will try to look down on folks for how they choose to live their own lives, relationship-wise. Adultery is called a work of the flesh (Galatians 5:19) and boy, if there is one thing that American Christians are gonna promote that is directly against Scripture, it's "following your heart". *What in the world?* In this context, the heart is defined as "the center of your emotions", and why you think you should follow something as fickle as those, the world will never know. Not only that but, "***The heart is deceitful above all things***, *and desperately wicked; Who can know it? I, the Lord, search the heart, I test the mind, even to give every man according to his ways, according to the fruit of his doings.*" (Jeremiah 17:9-10 — NKJV)

Therefore, it makes sense to a lot of Christians that they can cheat on God and it's all good, yet if their spouse cheats on them, they can just...move on to someone else. *Gee, and that represents covenant? Does it?* Because I recall God instructing Hosea to stay with his wife, Gomer, to show people what it was like for Jerusalem to continue to be unfaithful to Adonai. Yeah, don't also get me started on how much people's reactions to infidelity typically tend to be more about ego than anything else anyway because, really, you think that your spouse sleeping with someone else is the only way to be unfaithful in a marriage? *You can't be serious.* Some of y'all are unfaithful because you're *not* sleeping with your spouse enough. Scripture backs me on that:

"The husband should give to his wife her conjugal rights (goodwill, kindness, and what is due her as his wife), and likewise the wife to her husband. For the wife does not have [exclusive] authority and control over her own body, but the husband [has his rights]; likewise also the husband does not have [exclusive] authority and control over his body, but the wife [has her rights]. ***Do not refuse and deprive and defraud each other [of your due marital rights], except perhaps by mutual consent for a time, so that you may devote yourselves unhindered to prayer. But afterwards resume marital relations, lest Satan tempt you [to sin] through your lack of restraint of sexual desire****." (I Corinthians 7:3-5—AMPC)

I'm telling you, between Disney (some of y'all need to read up on the history of Walt Disney; his ultimate agenda too), rom-coms and how much people like to look at Scripture through rose-colored glasses, the perception of the purpose and commitment within marriage is beyond tainted. In my opinion, it has pretty much become perverse. Why do I say that? Because, if you claim to be a believer, your main reason for entering a marriage is to learn how to love like Christ does and his journey shows how his relationship with his bride was. If you've got any other (top) agenda in mind, marriage probably isn't for you. Besides, as I say often, if Adam and Eve could remain married, after doing something as life-altering as bringing sin into this world, most of y'all can figure out how to keep your vows too; especially since the Word also says:

"Do not be rash with your mouth, and let not your heart utter anything hastily before God. For God is in heaven, and you on earth; therefore, let your words be few. For a dream comes through much activity, and a fool's voice is known by his many words. **<u>When you make a vow to God, do not delay to pay it; for He has no pleasure in fools. Pay what you have vowed—better not to vow than to vow and not pay</u>***. Do not let your mouth cause your flesh to sin, nor say before the messenger of God that it was an error. Why should God be angry at your excuse and destroy the work of your hands? For in the multitude of dreams and many words there is also vanity. But fear God."* (Ecclesiastes 5:2-7 — NKJV)

You know, when Christ broke down just how serious marriage is in Matthew 19:1-12, his disciples' response was, *"The disciples said to Him, If the case of a man with his wife is like this, it is neither profitable nor advisable to marry."* (Matthew 19:10 — AMPC) That was after Christ explained who is not free to marry again after marriage. Hmph. *Disciples again, for the win.* While Christians are out here with multiple spouses, disciples are like, "If it's that serious, maybe it's wiser to remain single." I mean, if you're going to treat spouses like boyfriends or girlfriends and divorces like mere breakups and if you're not going to take covenant-keeping seriously and literally...yes, *single is just how you should remain.* It really can't be said enough that covenant-making and keeping are not for the weak, the fickle or those who like to romanticize things. Your word is to be your bond. If you don't have that kind of integrity or maturity — say nothing. VOW NOTHING. It's better to do that than make marriage your god instead of God (some of y'all will catch that later).

One more point on marriage before I move on, because, as I see more and more modern-day feminism coming from the pulpit (where is that biblically-backed, by the way?), if I hear one more woman say that, "I don't just have to submit to my husband; we are to submit to each other", I'm going to scream. *Literally.*

Man, I don't have enough time and space to get into all of this in this book of mine; however, in a nutshell, *submission is something that God put into place to restore the trust that was lost in the Garden of Eden.* Prior to sin, submission was not needed because — and please hear this loud and clear when I say this — when you are in agreement with someone, there's nothing to submit for or to. That said, when the Woman decided to listen to the Liar (the serpent — John 8:44) over the instructions that Adam imparted to her via God's direction (because with the way the story is told, it looks like that's how it went down — Genesis 3) and then Adam took the fruit too, the consequences were that Adam would have to struggle for provision and that, as far as the Woman was concerned, her husband would "rule" over her (and it would hurt to have children). No longer could the Woman, now Eve, go rogue; she would need some accountability in the form of submission. Colossians 3:18 speaks on it. Titus 2:5 speaks on it (that's where "obey" is). Ephesians 5:22-24 (NKJV) speaks on it: "***Wives, submit to your own husbands, as to the Lord.*** *For the husband is head of the wife, as also Christ is head of the church; and He is the Savior of the body. Therefore, just as the church is subject to Christ, so let the wives be to their own husbands in everything.*" When Ephesians 5:21 talks about "submit to one another", that is not referring to *marriage*; that is referring to *accountability*, in general — with people, in general.

And yes, a wife submitting to her husband as her husband submits to the Lord makes all of the sense in the world when you think about the fact that God gave Adam instructions and he decided to submit to his wife instead, while the Woman was told what God said to do by Adam and she decided to submit to the Liar instead. So, since neither of them were good with holding themselves accountable, God decided for restoration to happen by instructing Adam's sons to submit to Christ as Eve's daughters are to submit to their husband. Why this is so hard for people (outside of egomania and very poor biblical teaching), I have absolutely no clue. Submission helps to bring back a state of divine and sacred spiritual agreement, because, indeed, *"Can two walk together, unless they are agreed?"* (Amos 3:3 — NKJV) And so, yes, if all of this is too problematic or old-fashioned for you, *stay single*. Because, from a biblical standpoint, if a man doesn't trust the Lord enough to lead him, he doesn't need to get married, and if a woman doesn't trust the man she's seeing enough to lead her, she should do the same. *If* they follow Scripture, that is. *If* they want to be restored back to the Garden of Eden (so to speak), that is.

And yet, because Westernized Christians (because some of y'all need to remember that the Bible is Eastern-cultured; so is the Torah and the Quran) like to act like the Bible is some sort of pop culture manual, they like to "shift with the times" when the Word advises nothing of the sort (2 Timothy 3:16-17, Malachi 3:6, Psalm 119:89). Wives from biblical times were to submit to their husband. Wives from the *Little House on the Prairie* days were to submit to their husband. *Wives now are still supposed to submit to their husband*. Y'all can't Double Dutch on when traditionalism should matter. One day, you talk about it's "a man's role" to provide for you and the next day, you don't need to submit anymore because that is an antiquated notion (talk about being double-minded and the instability that comes with and from that — James 1:2-8). Some of y'all sound absolutely ridiculous. If you claim to follow Scripture, *follow it*. On the other hand, if you want to treat it like an emotional pamphlet, say that and stop acting like you're something that you're not: a believer, because if you're constantly editing verses to line up with society or to make you feel more comfortable, a believer of and in Scripture (and definitely a disciple), you are not.

OK, onto what helps to "fuel" marriage next...

You already saw that one of the people who I dedicated this book to is a woman by the name of Sarah Gaines. There's no time to get into all of the ways that Sarah was a dope individual, both in general and to me, personally. For now, I'll just say that for the last couple of years of her life, I would cut her hair. During those moments, we'd have really humorously fascinating conversations. Because she knew me since I was 21, we had many talks about each other's lives and so I knew that, after 30-plus years of marriage, her husband ended their covenant (well, on earthly terms anyway — some of y'all will catch that later). When I asked her if she was ever tempted to get married again (because she shared the same convictions on divorce and marrying another person while her former spouse was still alive as I do), she said something that had me rolling and feeling like, "See...*that's why* God wanted us to be virgins on our wedding night!" Sarah immediately said, "And have another penis inside of me? Yuck!" (She was such a covenant hero of mine, I tell you! Yeah, they don't make a lot of 'em like her anymore. It's a shame too.)

Preach, Sarah. I say it often: The way this culture dates, it teaches people how to divorce, not marry, and a part of that is because of sex. I say that because, if you are sexually active all throughout your dating journey, it's difficult to see things through Sarah's eyes; it's easier to not see marriage or sex as sacred — even though they both are indeed just that:

"There's more to sex than mere skin on skin. Sex is as much spiritual mystery as physical fact. As written in Scripture, 'The two become one.' Since we want to become spiritually one with the Master, we must not pursue the kind of sex that avoids commitment and intimacy, leaving us more lonely than ever—the kind of sex that can never 'become one.' There is a sense in which sexual sins are different from all others. In sexual sin we violate the sacredness of our own bodies, these bodies that were made for God-given and God-modeled love, for 'becoming one' with another. Or didn't you realize that your body is a sacred place, the place of the Holy Spirit? Don't you see that you can't live however you please, squandering what God paid such a high price for? The physical part of you is not some piece of property belonging to the spiritual part of you. God owns the whole works. So let people see God in and through your body." (I Corinthians 6:16-20 — Message)

Let me tell it, the Church SUCKS at teaching sex properly. Sure, it might tell single people not to do it while threatening them with fear about things like pregnancy, STIs/STDs and hell and damnation (umm, the same Bible that talks about the consequences of fornication offers the same consequences for adultery, and again, adultery ain't what most folks think that it is; y'all don't like to talk about *that*, though — I Corinthians 6:9-10, Hebrews 13:4), yet it doesn't really speak of *the purpose* of copulation in a way that would make more people want to wait until they are able to become physically one with their spouse. I say it often: when you don't know the purpose of something, you will almost always abuse/misuse it.

Take a newly married couple's wedding night, for example. Did you know that, reportedly, only around 48 percent of people actually have sex then? So, you've got all the time in the world to prioritize music, salmon plates and pictures, and yet, somehow, consummating your bond with your partner takes a back seat? Suddenly, you're "too tired" for that? Amazing. And honestly, a lot of people end up bringing that same lethargic "I'll get around to it" energy into their marriage bed (Hebrews 13:4) as well because they forget (or is it ignore?) the fact that consummate means "complete" and therefore, YOUR WEDDING DAY IS NOT COMPLETE WITHOUT HAVING SEX WITH YOUR PARTNER ON YOUR WEDDING NIGHT. Shoot, according to what I've read and researched in Hebrew culture, back in the day, couples would go into a room and their guests would have to wait for the reception to get started until *after* they came out "as one" — *that's how serious and important consummating was.* And so, sex helps to complete marriage; it is a part of the "becoming one process". It is the top priority of the act because, think about it: Adam and his Woman had sex in the Garden, pre-sin, and yet didn't have children until after leaving the Garden, post-sin. Yes, cultivating and celebrating oneness is the first goal, aim, mission of sexual activity.

It goes deeper than that, though. Hands down, one of my favorite Scriptures is the part of I Corinthians 6 that I just referenced. It's packed with so much wisdom. Indeed, sex is not just a physical act, a way of "getting off" that our culture seems so obsessed with; there are also many spiritual mysteries that transpire during the process too. I dig that because a mystery is a revelation — and that is one of the reasons why I tell a lot of my married clients that they should have sex as often as possible (reportedly, people in healthy marriages have sex at least once a week); it's because there is absolutely no telling what kind of revelations that they will receive when they do. Scripture says so.

Another thing about sex? It helps to reduce stress, increases pleasure hormones like dopamine and it helps you to bond more with your partner via other hormones like oxytocin; this means that it does wonders for you physically as well. Hmm and while we're here on the physical tip, I remember hearing a pastor and his wife say from the pulpit that it is wrong to engage in oral sex. Chile. So...what did they learn in school that a cistern is, because my dictionary says that it's "a reservoir, tank, or container for storing or holding water or other liquid" *and* that it's "a reservoir or receptacle of some natural fluid of the body". Meanwhile, the Bible that I read says things like, *"Drink water from your own cistern, and running water from your own well"* (Proverbs 5:15 — NKJV) — and the context of this is coming from a chapter of the Bible that warns about adultery. Not only that but if you do research on the benefits of fellatio (and the act of unprotected sex, in general, thanks to the contents of sperm and semen), wives are able to have better moods and less depression; prettier skin; stronger hair; less menstrual cramps; a boost in their cognitive abilities; an improved chance of longevity, and even a lower risk of preeclampsia while pregnant...and that's just for starters. For guys, cunnilingus is the ultimate probiotic (due to what's in vaginal fluid). No joke. Look it up.

When a husband and wife have sex, spiritual revelations are revealed, and their health significantly improves. Now, how often do you hear *anything* about this in your church? Here Scripture states that husbands and wives are to be "naked and NOT ashamed" (Genesis 2:24-25), meanwhile, church folks are out here acting like sex should be a taboo topic. *Y'all should be <u>ashamed</u> for acting that way.*

Something else? Don't even get me on the Hebrew meaning of "yada, yada, yada". Did you know that it means "to know" on an intimate level? OK, and what does the (New) King James Version frame sex between a married couple to be? KNOWING EACH OTHER, right? Genesis 4:1(NKJV) is a good example: *"**<u>Now Adam knew Eve his wife,</u>** and she conceived and bore Cain, and said, 'I have acquired a man* *from the Lord.'"* To know someone is to be fully aware of them, to understand them, to experience them. When you engage in sexual activity with your partner, it is designed to help you to get to KNOW them more and better. And since, according to Scripture, sex is only for married couples, the act is supposed to help you to know your spouse in a way that no one else should. Something else that's dope about yada, yada, yada and knowing? Some scholars say that the same kind of knowing that the Lord has of us in Psalm 139 is the same kind of knowing that a husband and his wife should seek to obtain, in part, through the act of sex. Hmph. Again, let me tell it, a lot of these couples who divorce, all the while claiming that they don't "know each other anymore", ask them how often they *knew each other* up in that bedroom of theirs. Yeah, that's why I adore another verse in Scripture when it comes to sex; one that is very simple and a lot of people don't catch: *"Behold, you are handsome, my beloved! Yes, pleasant!* **_Also, our bed is green_**" (Song of Solomon 1:16 — NKJV). Green symbolizes things like health, prosperity, fertility, growth, balance, freshness and rejuvenation. No wonder babies are conceived through the act of sex. Just look at how beautiful and miraculous sex is!

And before some of y'all start — you know, some of you semi-miserable sexless married people who try and justify not prioritizing sex, which is biblically disobedient, by the way — *again*, read I Corinthians 7:5. *Age is no excuse*. In fact, Google just how much sex seniors are having sex. It's running circles around a ton of you, oral sex included! For instance, reportedly, over half of elders between 75-85 get it in 2-3 times a month and about that same amount partake in fellatio and cunnilingus as well. Because, again, Adam and his wife didn't make babies in perfection. Oh, but they had sex, though. Bottom line, sex should start a marriage and, so long as two people are physically capable, it should continue until death parts them too. It's a profound-ly intricate act (I mean, a clitoris literally only exists so that women can have orgasms; God covered all of the bases) that is designed to CELEBRATE LOVE, not "make" it.

I've got one more covenant principle to get into, so I've got to wrap this part up; however, I do need to say why I discern that sex prior to marriage is frowned upon by God. It's not because he doesn't want us to experience pleasure (c'mon now); it's because the weight of sex is quite layered and it shouldn't be used/abused to create/make something that should already exist before two people come together (not to mention that it shouldn't be an act that "starts and stops" based on what happens while dating; it is to last for the rest of our lives — continually so). Yeah, I have always hated the phrase "make love". When someone has signed up to, as a husband, provide for and protect a woman for the rest of her life or, as a wife, help and nurture a man for the rest of his life, sex isn't "making" anything — y'all, sex is *amplifying* something. It's like two people are coming together to say, "Babe, come here and let me remind you of something special about you and us"...again, and again and again. Until death parts them.

And for those of you who think that you need to inquire about why I write and talk about sex so much — you know what? Coming from the generations of divorce that I do and the amount of sexual abuse and misuse that I experienced, I get why Satan (and his cheer-leaders, because some of y'all work for him whether you realize it or not) didn't want me to get to this point and place in my purpose and life, in general. In fact, something my mother used to say often is Satan hates me, and I think a part of it is because he knows that both he and I actually see the value of marriage and sex far more than most humans do, including a ton of Christians. And so, until I leave this earth, speaking of the things that I study and research as it relates to marriage and sex will be what I do, aggressively and incessantly so, because they are covenant principles that the Church is *absolutely not* doing a good job of teaching or modeling on a billion different levels. Covenant is nothing to be quiet about, ignorant on or ashamed of. Not by any stretch of the imagination. Some of y'all are buggin'. Not to mention that *"My people are destroyed for lack of knowledge. Because you have rejected knowledge..."* (Hosea 4:6 — NKJV), and it's hard to do well what you have limited knowledge on.

And with *that* said, just one more covenant principle to go.

Oh, the Sabbath. When it comes to this particular topic, if there are two things that I don't get about Christians, it's 1) how do we all agree that Christ rose on Sunday and Matthew 28:1 says that it is the first day of the week (while the Sabbath is the seventh one — Exodus 20:8-11) and 2) how y'all claim to be followers of Christ when honoring the Sabbath was his custom and he is literally the Lord of the Sabbath (Luke 6:5)? Really, let's go even deeper than that: in the Garden of Eden, God, the One who never sleeps or slumbers (Psalm 121:4), he actually rested on the Sabbath: *"Then God blessed the seventh day and sanctified it, because in it He rested from all His work which God had created and made"* (Genesis 2:3 — NKJV) In fact, one of the things that I tell first-day folks (you know, those who act like Sunday is the Sabbath when it absolutely is not) often is, "Y'all need to be careful with all of that rippin' and runnin' that you do on the Sabbath. God has already said that he slows down on that day." *I mean, did he not?*

In fact, that's actually what Shabbat means: to cease from creating, and the Fourth Commandment makes it clear what that should look like:

"Remember the Sabbath day, to keep it holy. Six days you shall labor and do all your work, but the seventh day is the Sabbath of the Lord your God. In it you shall do no work: you, nor your son, nor your daughter, nor your male servant, nor your female servant, nor your cattle, nor your stranger who is within your gates. For in six days the Lord made the heavens and the earth, the sea, and all that is in them, and rested the seventh day. Therefore, the Lord blessed the Sabbath day and hallowed it." (Exodus 20:8-11 — NKJV)

We are to keep the Sabbath day holy, not work and bless and hallow it; hallow means consecrated and set apart. In other words, the Sabbath day is not to be treated like every other day; it is especially special (kind of like all of your money belongs to God, yet 10 percent is to be "set apart" — Malachi 3:10, Proverbs 3:9-10).

And for the skeptics — or people who want to act like they don't know how to count — how else can we know, for sure, when the Sabbath is? I mean, again, Christ was a Jew, right? *When do Jews keep it — still?* From Friday sunset to Saturday sunset is the answer. And why is that? Because a creation day is "evening and morning" (reread Genesis 1). And why should *you* still keep it? Because Christ did. Now, did Christ show the Pharisees how to keep it better? 1000 percent (some Adventists who are Sabbath keepers may have the right day, yet they certainly have light years to go on how to honor it better). However, did he ever tell us to dismiss it or shift it to another day? AB-SOLUTELY NOT and since Christ was once documented as saying things like *"If you love Me, keep My commandments"* (John 14:15 — NKJV) and *"He who has My commandments and keeps them, it is he who loves Me. And he who loves Me will be loved by My Father, and I will love him and manifest Myself to him"* (John 14:21 — NKJV), well, I'm not sure how it can get any clearer than that. ALL COMMANDMENTS ARE STILL RELEVANT.

Besides, first-day folks tend to tickle me as they "fight to not rest", anyway. Again, most of the ones I know, they are the busiest on Saturdays. Then they go to church on Sunday and before they know it — ding! — here is Monday again. Imagine if you actually got off of the grid (so to speak) on Friday evening, *rested on Sabbath* (because you Adventists being in church all day, I doubt that is what Scripture had in mind either) and then you used Sunday to ease into your work week? Because, above all else, that is what the Sabbath is for: REST. How many Christians actually do that, though? Not many.

A Hebrew word for rest is *"menuchah"*. One of the things that it means is to "rest in the love that is freely given" and "rest in a state of peace and serenity". The true Sabbath is supposed to provide this for us. The Sabbath also marks the end of creation and so, all of the things that we did during the other six days of the week, the Sabbath is designed to allow us to not just "pause" from our labor but look back and celebrate what we've accomplished (overthinkers and work-aholics definitely need the Sabbath!). A reason why I know it is a part of my own calling is because the Sabbath is also a covenant principle; the Ten Commandments, period, are a part of the covenant, and no, it is not an "old law" that was "done away" with. In 2 Timothy 3:16-17(NKJV), it literally says that "***All Scripture is given by inspiration of God***, *and is profitable for doctrine, for reproof, for correction, for instruction in righteousness, that the man of God may be complete, thoroughly equipped for every good work*" and the Sabbath is report-edly mentioned somewhere around 172 times; close to 60 of those being in the New Testament. Wanna know something else? According to the Talmud (a great source of Jewish law and theology), once upon a time, rabbis used to dress up in white as a representation of being God's bride on the Sabbath, marking a special time of intimacy with him. So, while Sunday folks are out here basically doing what they want to do as far as the Sabbath is concerned (even if you say that you are treating Sunday as the Sabbath to celebrate Christ's resurrection, there is not one Scripture that instructs you to do that), by really diving into the significance of the true Sabbath and the Hebrew thoughts and customs surrounding it, you can get why observing it on the day that the Bible instructs, will always be necessary and relevant. Divine rest, as God tells us to do it, will always be significantly supreme.

*"And He said, 'My Presence will go with you, **and I will give you rest**"* (Exodus 33:14 — NKJV)

*"Come to Me, all you who labor and are heavy laden, **and I will give you rest**"* (Matthew 11:28 — NKJV)

The Sabbath? It is one of the ways that the Lord gives us rest. It is a commandment, yes. In fact, back in the Old Testament, not observing the Sabbath was oftentimes punishable by death, and that is because not walking in agreement with the Lord by honoring ALL of his covenant brought forth that consequence. To see how so many Christians now water down the importance of covenant-keeping, when it comes to the Sabbath and, again, marriage and sex — one more time for the backseats and stubborn folks, Scripture literally asks, *"Can two walk together, unless they are agreed?"* (Amos 3:3 — NKJV) God never asked what we thought or how we felt about his covenant-based instructions; he simply told us to follow them — point, blank, and period. And the super sad thing is, folks would rather do what's popular (when the Message Version of Luke 6:26 tells us to do what's rooted in truth over what is popular), what their grandmama and mama did/does (Black folks, some of y'all need to study how much you are doing based on what slave masters taught, keeping in mind that many of them had problems with not just us but Jews), what is convenient or easy instead of honoring and abiding by what covenant literally means.

And what ultimately is that? A Hebrew word for covenant is "b'riyt". It means "to select the best." People who are serious about walking with God and honoring his covenant are ultimately saying that they want to do whatever it takes to have the best in life, so that they can ultimately have the best in the afterlife too. And for me, what an honor it has been and continues to be, to be a mouthpiece for that — to remind individuals to "select the best" when it comes to a life partner (probably the most important decision you will make in life is who you choose to marry), the quality of intimacy that you choose to experience with that individual, and resting on the day that GOD ORDAINED (and there is only one).

My name means covenant.

I was born in the season of covenant.

My purpose teaches about covenant.

And it's all about putting THE BEST over everything else.

Gee, God, it all has truly come together. I thank you.

"If you have to forgive someone almost 500 times for the same offense, both of you have not learned your lesson."

(SHELLIE R. WARREN VIA THE HOLY SPIRIT)

Chapter Eleven
Victims Should Forgive.
Victimizers Should Repent...
Oh, and Then Some.

In the midst of reading an excerpt from a couple of chapters of my book to a friend of mine, he said, "You're not just word-literal; you are WORD-literal." LOL. I mean, at least I try to be, so that was high praise; especially coming from him (he's a minister). I think that's another reason why I just don't fit in with Christian folks; it's because there are so many things that they do that absolutely baffle me — Word-wise... so many things that aren't Word-based and yet they seem to think that because they say some variation of, "Thank God for grace", that somehow makes it alright.

Take worshipping Christ, for example. *Where in the Bible does it tell us to do that?* Meanwhile, Christians will teach their kids to pray, "Dear Jesus", when Christ clearly told us to start out prayers with, *"Our Father in heaven, hallowed be your name."* (Matthew 6:9) Christians will act like there is not a hierarchy in the Godhead, when clearly there is one; otherwise, Christ would know when he is returning (and he doesn't — Matthew 24:36) and I Corinthians 11:3 (NKJV) wouldn't say, *"But I want you to know that the head of every man is Christ, the* *head of woman is man, **and the head of Christ is God**.*" Christians constantly talk as if Christ is here right now, when the Word says things like, "*My Father's house has many rooms; if that were not so, would I have told you that I am going there to prepare a place for you? **And if I go and prepare a place for you, I will come back and take you to be with me that you also may be where I am**. You know the way to the place where I am going*" (John 14:2-4 — NIV) and "*If you [really] love Me, you will keep (obey) My commands. **And I will ask the Father, and He will give you another Comforter (Counselor, Helper, Intercessor, Advocate, Strengthener, and Standby), that He may remain with you forever**—the Spirit of Truth, Whom the world cannot receive (welcome, take to its heart), because it does not see Him or know and recognize Him. But you know and recognize Him, for He lives with you [constantly] and will be in you.*" (John 14:15-17 — AMPC) Yeah, the way that so much of the Church acts like the Holy Spirit only shows up, for the most part, at altar calls is really something else. Anyway, so is Christ our Savior? Yes. (I John 4:14). Is he Adonai? No, he is not. Whew, it's another message for another time that folks would be able to better understand the concept of Godhead (I liken it to ice, water and steam) if people actually did marital covenant in a more excellent way — because, yes, you can be separate beings who are united in the same purpose. It's marriage that was supposed to model that (I John 5:8, Genesis 2:24-25). Anyway, let me get to the second thing that I think is a trip among the brethren before I lose my focus: *expecting victims to do more work than victimizers when it comes to restoring relationships.*

There is a relatively new show out right now called *Unprisoned* that, although I haven't watched it (perhaps yet), I did see a commercial for it; one that contained a liner that I wish I had jotted down so that I could share it verbatim. Basically, a teenager asked his mom why it made sense to her that she is like her own dad while she seemed to not get how he can play the same card when it comes to being like her (preach, chile). The spin that I will put on that, as it relates to this topic is, isn't it interesting that when (for example) a family member hurts, harms or offends one of their relatives, oftentimes, they are quick to bring up the things that happened to them, things that were passed down generationally (as if to justify why *they chose* to treat you a certain way) — oh, but let you be struggling with those same generational curses and suddenly they don't get it and you need to simply stop. Or those very same people will tell you that they haven't forgiven someone who has harmed them, and yet when they turn around and harm you, it being a challenge to pardon them suddenly makes no sense to them at all. See the gaslighting? See the manipulation? So, you are out here jacking up lives due to some relative or former spouse or whatever and yet the damage *you've* done, folks should just automatically understand and forgive? *Just because you think or say so?* Simply because you are uncomfortable with dealing with the fallout of the harm you've actually caused? Humans are something else, boy.

Does that mean don't forgive them? I mean, spiritually, you should. Science actually backs it up, too, because people who harbor unforgivingness typically have more stress; tend to deal with more anxiety and depression-related symptoms; have a weaker immune system; are at a greater risk for heart disease, and they tend to have bouts of insomnia. OK, but what does it mean to forgive? Word-wise, I mean. Because now that we're coming close to the end of this 20-year update, clearly, there is a lot of forgiveness that has needed to transpire in my own life; of that, I am aware. Well, although I didn't go into writing this book thinking that it would be as Word-heavy as it turned out to be, it is a big part of who I am, so let's break it down from that point, place and space.

A Hebrew word for forgive is *"salahh"* (there are variations in spelling). It roughly means "lift up" in the sense of removing something. Although I didn't know it at the time, when I decided to shift from "cutting people off" to "releasing them" — I think that I was bringing the spirit of salahh into my space, being that it is similar to that: release the hurt, harm or pain, so that you can move forward with your life. Some other definitions include to pardon or to spare in the sense of not giving people what they actually deserve. Uh-huh, some folks really need to get that: that when people don't give you what you truly deserve, that *is* a form of forgiveness (I mean, some of you REALLY need to get that). Let's keep going.

If you look at "forgive" from the angle of biblical instruction, Matthew 6:14-15 (NKJV) is pretty crystal clear: *"For if you forgive people their trespasses [their reckless and willful sins, leaving them, letting them go, and giving up resentment], your heavenly Father will also forgive you. But if you do not forgive others their trespasses [their reckless and willful sins, leaving them, letting them go, and [f]giving up resentment], neither will your Father forgive you your trespass-es."* And honestly, this makes all of the sense in the world. Because, indeed, it would be pretty arrogant (not to mention, totally delusional) to think that you should be forgiven by God for things that you do as you withhold that same mercy when it comes to what people do to you (by the way, I'm pretty sure this is just one of the reasons why God hates divorce; it's because it is quite the act of unforgivingness, whether people choose to see it that way or not). So yeah, if you want to receive this type of gift from the Lord, you've got to give what you'd like to have; it's like a spiritual form of reciprocity (in a way). However, what Christ spoke of here is what's needed to get and be right with him. HIM.

As far as *reconciliation* goes, there are a few things that need to take place on *the victimizer's part* — and that's what always trips me out. As far as the victimizer goes, folks (especially church folks) tend to expect more from the victim (which I'm sure has something to do with that spiritual narcissism thing again). Oh, and as far as spectators of what has transpired (or they think has transpired) go, all they end up doing is *revictimizing the victim* by cramming the importance of forgiveness down their throat when they tend to have very little of the story and/or no idea the pain that was actually caused. I'm telling you, the longer that I live on this earth, the more I get that in this world, when it comes to dealing with people, nine times out of 10, before saying or doing anything, you should ask yourself if you are on your way to hurting or harming the — no matter what your "intentions" may be. And if someone has been hurt or harmed by someone else and here you come injecting your two cents with limited intel? Guess what? Helping them, you are absolutely not.

Besides, you — I'm still talking to spectators right now — have no idea if the person has forgiven or not, just because they may not be interacting with, engaging or in relationship with someone. Now, for the record, I will say that I know an individual who used to say all of the time that "forgiveness does not mean fellowship". Although I got her point, I must say that I never fully agreed with her. To me, it sounded like low-key weaponizing forgiveness. Plus, imagine if God was that way with us; imagine if he was on some, "I mean, I forgive you, but that doesn't mean that I'm about to roll with you like that." Yeah, it really is kind of wildly selfish and hypocritical how much folks want forgiveness and yet will pretty much power trip over granting it to others. And, indeed, if you want to see true evidence of someone having a peak level of self-awareness and spiritual maturity, peep their ability to forgive and how they are able to "connect" with those who they have forgiven after the fact.

Uh-huh. And if some of you are thinking, "Interesting coming from you, Shellie," considering that I'm estranged from so much of my family, I totally get it. Let's keep going before you draw any extreme conclusions, though.

For one thing, forgiveness is typically a process. Oh, and that brings me to something else about church culture that irks me to absolutely no end. Just like baptism is a public display of a commitment that one has already made to God, altar calls should be seen as a way of someone taking accountability for whatever they feel their particular area of weakness is at the time. HOWEVER (and yes, I am absolutely yelling this!), that doesn't automatically or necessarily mean that they don't have a ton of self-work to do once they walk away from it. Yeah, I can't tell you how many folks go down to the altar who have serious issues that need medication and/or therapy, all the while assuming that nothing else is required, as they walk away from that space. Sadly, that broken way of thinking/believing is just what keeps them in a straight-up cyclic state. Well, along those same lines, forgiveness can be similar.

Personally, one of my favorite definitions of forgiveness is by best-selling author, Gary Zukav. According to him, "Forgiveness is accepting that the past cannot change" and that really is the truth. At the end of the day, no matter how much someone may regret what they did, they can't go back and change it and the person they did it to needs to accept that fact (if they want to forgive, that is). At the same time, though, if someone really gets the impact and magnitude of the harm that they caused, they should get that oftentimes, again, *forgiveness is a process*. They need to give people space and time to fully accept that the past cannot change, along with the freedom to decide what they want to do about that reality. Backing up and giving them the space that they need — not the space that the offender thinks that the offendee should have — is only one step in all of this, though.

The next thing that needs to be done is FULL REPENTANCE (Matthew 3). Not a flippant, "my bad". Not a, what my molester initially did (not realizing that I had been shown some of the journals that confirmed so much of what was done to me), which was, "If that's what you think that I did, I apologize." Dude, you can so keep that. Not an "I've already said that I'm sorry. I'm not going to apologize again." Umm, people who think that these are a genuine form of an apology sound straight-up nuts. They also sound like they are just throwing words out there to get on with matters. And really, if this is how you get down, why should anyone trust you, pretty much at all, if you apologize like that? You know, one definition of repent is "to feel sorry, self-reproachful, or contrite for past conduct" while another is "regret or be conscience-stricken about a past action, attitude, etc." When it comes to my personal journey with this family tree of mine, I can count on less than one hand the people who felt contrite or conscience-stricken about all of the balls that they dropped in my life while growing up. Honestly, it's a very slim amount who even said, "I'm sorry" (my grandparents and godparents are truly a trip in this area). And so, if you aren't bothered by what you did to begin with and/or you have too much pride to thoroughly address it (without selective memory or gaslighting, please), why should we be in relationship with one another? Pretty much, you are a dangerous individual to be around because you are out here just being reckless and not feeling bad about it — by mere definition of the word "repent".

OK, so what about the people who did say "I'm sorry"....like my mom? Because, to be fair, she has said it many times over the years. Well, for one thing, "I'm sorry" means very little if you keep on doing the same type of stuff that you are apologizing for in the first place. Hmph, that reminds me — I'll never forget a time when I was writing a devotional on forgiveness and, when I referenced the biblical story of Christ telling someone to forgive "seventy times seven" (Matthew 18:21-25), in my head, even as I was writing it, I was like, "490 times?!" Now, guess what the Holy Spirit said to me in response: "If you've got to forgive someone almost 500 times for the same offense, both of you haven't learned their lesson." INDEED. And *that* reminds me of something that I once heard a man by the name of Cedric Dent say, many years ago, during a Sabbath school class about forgiveness: "If I tell you a secret, you share it and then ask for forgiveness, I'll forgive you; that doesn't mean that I am going to tell you any more secrets any time soon, though. It's not because I don't forgive you. It's because you have shown me that you are weak in the area of confidentiality and so, that is my way of holding you accountable." *Right.* Saying "I'm sorry" only to turn around and do the same things over...and over... and over again? Listen, *if you, as the offender, will not shift, I, as the offendee must* — because you are actually *tempting me* to no longer forgive you, which ultimately puts my own walk with God in jeopardy. Yep, if you choose to not hold yourself accountable, I will, because forgiving you doesn't mean that there aren't consequences for your actions. *God forgives us and there are consequences all of the time.* God forgave my abortions. Life played out that I won't have any more kids, though. Maturity teaches you to accept the reaping that comes with your sowing, even if you've been pardoned for the seeds that you planted in the first place.

OK, so what about the fact that Scripture says that we are called to the "ministry of reconciliation"? Well, for one thing, most of the sub-headings for 2 Corinthians 5:12-21 (where that is referenced) speaks of reconciling oneself *to God*. However, because unity and harmony are heavenly concepts, I'll play along. The thing about reconciliation is, if the offender is serious about that transpiring with the person who they hurt, they need to take several steps beyond mere lip service. Oh, and this is where you can tell if trust is truly capable of being restored (again, over time and absolutely not on the victimizer's clock because, to try and force someone's healing is just another form of harming them), because if you want to heal a relationship, if you want to prove that you get at least some level of what you've done, you will seek to make an amends — *and* you will atone for what has transpired.

Amends: reparation or compensation for a loss, damage, or injury of any kind; recompense; improvement; recovery, as of health.

Atone: to make amends or reparation, as for an offense or a crime, or for an offender; to make up, as for errors or deficiencies (usually followed by for); to become reconciled; agree.

If there's one thing that my blood relatives can vouch for when it comes to me, it's that I'm gonna call some things flat-out, address uncomfortable issues and ask some deep questions (sue us; that's just how curse-breakers roll). So, when I (for instance) confronted my maternal grandfather about the trauma that he caused my mom and the rest of his immediate family (I was in my 20s at the time), all he did was throw Scripture around, out of context. Chile, bye. My paternal grandfather? As I've said before, I respect him for how candid he was about how much he dropped the ball on my dad and ultimately myself. He didn't apologize, though. Not to me, anyway. My paternal grandmother? She was such a prideful and bitter woman (whew, she complained a lot) that it was hard to take her too seriously; definitely mentally and emotionally unsafe on a billion different levels (my dad had stories for days). And I'm using these three people as examples because, in these instances, I was the child — and no, *a child shouldn't have to do more work to maintain a relationship, let alone mend one, than adults should*. If my grandparents had chosen (because it is indeed a choice) to reconcile, they would've repented, made an amends and atoned. Simple as that.

Now, to be fair, there were drizzled amends as far as my paternal grandfather was concerned. Although he didn't call, there were $50 Christmas checks. Although there was absolutely no proof of my father or my existence in his house (I went several times over the years), he did come up for a signing of my first book. I never saw him at a graduation or special event in my world and I doubt that he can give you even five facts about me as a person (that man might not even know my middle name), though. And you already read about how ludicrous the handling of my father's passing was — so, what is there to reconcile? For whatever the reason, you choose to not fully see the magnitude of the damage that has been done and it's evident based on the lack of amending and atoning you've done, so...we're good. Yes, I've forgiven you; I also remain out of your potential harm's way, so that you can't keep giving me reasons to forgive you in the same areas over and over again as well.

Because I'll tell you what — remember how I said in an earlier chapter that the way that I am repenting, amending and atoning for aborting my children is living out a part of their purpose, via their names, every single day? Lord, that is the absolute least that I can do for them. And honestly, becoming a doula is another way of making an amends and atoning. Sometimes, amending and atoning take a while, based on whatever offense was committed. And you know what? People who are truly sorry? They really get that. When the pain is deep, making amends and atoning must go deeper. True and genuine repentance gets that.

Another example is the former friend Adriel from another chapter. She always had a habit of looking to me for insight and comfort when she was hurting. Oh, but when she pulled a huge stunt and I told her, explicitly, how passive-aggressive and mean-spirited it was along with how it hurt me (via an email), she said nothing. No repenting. No amending. No atoning. I've seen her since. I know that I've forgiven her because I am able to speak and genuinely ask how she is (and semi-care). Is she a safe space, though? *Absolutely not.* Listen, we can — and should — forgive unsafe people; that does not mean that we have to be in intimate relationships with them, though... not when repenting, amending and atoning have not transpired. Why? Because, again, if they aren't willing to acknowledge what they have done, it's a pretty fair bet that they will repeat it — whatever "it" may be — on some level. It's through the act of amending and atoning that we find ourselves putting in so much effort in the restoration process that we don't even want to do what required those acts again...*ever.*

...

And so, that is why I am in perfect peace with where things stand with so many of the humans in the form of characters in my book. By not seeking to give them what they deserve, by pardoning their offenses enough to not be angry, bitter or desiring a way to "get back at them", by releasing them in the sense of allowing God and time to do whatever needs to be done — they *are* forgiven; it's not worth it to put my purpose, health or healthy relationships with others in jeopardy just because of other people's actions. At the same time, I will not do the work of amending and atoning, though — *that's for them to do.* Besides, the other thing about reconciliation is sometimes you need to be clear about if you are to be connected to certain people or — and please catch this — if you ever should've been, in the way that you were, in the first place, because, when it comes to me? PTSD Shellie selected some individuals that Real Shellie never would have. And as far as who I couldn't choose, my family — I tolerated things, in my PTSD state, that I never would now. On any level and for any reason.

Whew, it's so wild that, oftentimes, it's the very people with a victimizing spirit who think that reconnecting to them should be automatic when you may have never needed to be intimately involved with them to begin with OR you are at a place in your journey where being connected now would be a hindrance or supreme disservice. How people choose to amend and atone reveals a lot. So does time apart from them. That said, reconciliation should be a thoughtful and purposeful act — not just a practice that ultimately encourages cyclic patterns and habits.

And that is how I know, beyond a shadow of a doubt, that it was time for this book to be birthed. Again, with 20 (biblically) meaning "patience in waiting", I have been able to pen all of this from a place of forgiveness and releasing (chile, if you thought this was a wild ride, you have no idea what PTSD Shellie's version would be out here looking like). I am clear about what I needed to do. I know what I should require from others. It is well with my soul.

FINALLY. COMPLETELY. SELAH. AMEN.

"This is what you shall do:
Love the earth and sun and the animals,
despise riches, give alms to everyone that asks,
stand up for the stupid and crazy,
devote your income and labor to others,
hate tyrants, argue not concerning God,
have patience and indulgence toward the people,
take off your hat to nothing known or unknown
or to any man or number of men,
go freely with powerful uneducated persons
and with the young and with the mothers of families,
read these leaves in the open air every season
of every year of your life, re-examine all you have
been told at school or church or in any book,
dismiss whatever insults your own soul,
and your very flesh shall be a great poem
and have the richest fluency not only in its words
but in the silent lines of its lips and face and
between the lashes of your eyes and
in every motion and joint of your body."

(WALT WHITMAN)

Chapter Twelve
So, Here Are 20 Things
That the Past Twenty 20 Years
Have Taught Me...

Although I wrote a lot of the content for this book while I was 49, some of its "birthing" came right after I officially turned 50. And although I don't do holidays (however, I do dig the story of St. Valentine being martyred for marrying Christians in the sense of him bucking the system for the sake of covenant), if there's one day when I'm going to be extra, borderline obnoxious, and whatever other term that you wanna use, it's going to be my birthday. This means that you already know that 50? C'mon...*it's 50.* The year of jubilee. The time of Pentecost. A number that represents things like freedom, renewal and the literal manifestation of God's promises. Yeah, while some of y'all are scared to tell people your age, I was "rounding off" and saying that I was 50 before it officially even arrived!

And my tribe? Boy, did they show up and out for the occasion in some really thoughtful ways. I do think I have a favorite memory, though. It came from a male friend of mine who took me out for a belated birthday dinner; one that wasn't cheap by any stretch. When I arrived, the table had cards all over it (ones that I thought were a part of the table décor at first). I asked him if he wanted me to open them up immediately and he said that it was up to me. And so, I decided to do so after dinner.

There were five cards — all very thoughtful, message specific and visually beautiful. I'm a words of affirmation (and then physical touch) type of person, so he already won in my book. Yet when I opened the cards, each had $100 in them. *What in the world, my friend?*

Something that he and I have in common is biblical wisdom. Even at his lowest points, he's gonna find himself preaching on some level (LOL). And so, he started to speak some things into my life. One thing that stood out, especially, was when he said, "You deserve to know that we see you, Shellie. And with all that you've overcome, you deserve to be seen."

It's such a blessing to finally have safe people in my space. People who accept me just as I am — as they encourage me to become the best version of that (the right folks love you *and* hold you account-able; not either/or…BOTH). People who don't revictimize me by trying to minimize or gaslight me out of my past abuse and pain (one time, the nice guy narcissist told me that, when I decided to take some steps back from my mother to heal, that I was "being petty"; that is an unsafe response and he is an unsafe person for me); people who know my boundaries and respect them without trying to talk me out of them or be dismissive about them; people who see my purpose and celebrate it; people who really and truly "get me"…because they want to and choose to — on the regular.

Anyway, I would say this person's name; however, that would cause me to contradict what I've already stated as far as protecting my circle goes. He's already heard a lot of what's in this book (because he was a safe enough space to share it with); *he knows who he is*. And as I get to the point and place of wrapping this 20-year "So, what are you on now, Shellie?" update, I thought that memorializing what he did, in book form, would be a great way to intro this chapter — because "50" is a new season for me, in every way. And the woman I am now, by such a special group of carefully selected individuals, I am seen. *Really and truly seen.* As Nigerian author Chimamanda Ngozi Adichie once said, "Lasting love has to be built on mutual regard and respect. It is about seeing the other person." Loved, in a way where I finally feel loved, I am.

And so, although I know that I've gotten kinda deep into some of the things that "I am on" in this season of my life, as a way of commemorating my time between 29 and 49, I also want to share 20 other things that life and time have taught me; especially since *Inside of Me* was "birthed" back in 2004.

Things like what? In no particular order of importance (well, except for the first one):

1. GOD DOES NOT OWE US ANYTHING — and yes, I am yelling it! I can't tell you how many times I've watched people fractionate their relationship with the Lord and it was all because they have believed that they were *asking* him for something (or one) when they were actually attempting to *tell* him what to do, usually under the self-manipulation that, "God said he would give me the desires of my heart, so....". Uh-huh. The same Bible that says in Psalm 37:4 (you should remember to include the part that comes before that line, by the way) also says: *"You lust and do not have. You murder and covet and cannot obtain. You fight and war. Yet you do not have because you do not ask. You ask and do not receive, because you ask amiss, that you may spend it on your pleasures."* (James 4:2-3 — NKJV) The sooner you get that anything God does, or

doesn't do, is ultimately for your good, the less stressed (and entitled) you will feel...and the easier life becomes.

2. *Compromise your purpose for absolutely no one.* In fact, anyone who tries to get you off of what you know your purpose to be, they are an enemy, not an ally, of everything about you — relative, loved one, friend or not.

3. The wrong things in life will try to *change* you; the right things will seek to *improve* you. And yes, there is a difference between the two. Controlling people typically want to change you into who they think you should be/become. When you're around healthy individuals, you end up improving for the better, just by their mere presence.

4. Something that I currently have in a signature of one of my emails is this: "If your mind, body and spirit are not in agreement...pause." It's not a quote that I read; it's a motto that I made up and currently live by. I mentioned in another chapter that we each have a human trinity that is made up of our mind, body and spirit. If you're trying to figure out if something is right, good or wrong for you (by the way, always prioritize right over good; something can be good and still not what is best for your life), ask yourself if "your trinity" is working in harmony. If it's not, that's a red flag. This is truly one of life's greatest hacks. Trust me.

5. You don't deserve something (or one) just because *you* think that you do; believing otherwise is a huge form of en-titlement. Deserve, by definition, is "to qualify for". In other words, *be what you think that you deserve*...the work it takes to get there will humble you: *"By humility and the fear of the*

Lord are riches and honor and life." (Proverbs 22:4 — NKJV) It will cause you to be more patient and tolerant as well.

6. Women don't have a lock on intuition. Also, intuition that is attached to ego is typically nothing more than arrogant presumption. How some of these folks out here are doing things based on intuition without applying self-awareness and common sense truly boggles the mind. By the way, check out the Message Version of Proverbs 2 sometime. It'll bless ya.

7. Puzzle pieces don't have to force their fit; in the "pictures" they belong in, they apply comfortably and easily (some of you will catch that later).

8. If there is no reciprocity, while you may be in "something", it is not a relationship — and definitely not a healthy one. Figure out if it's ministry (service), a seasonal offer of support or if you're in a toxic dynamic. No one who truly cares about you is going to be comfortable being in a situation where all they are doing is receiving and not giving.

9. Maturity teaches you to choose the people, places, things and ideas that will truly complement your life; not just who and/or what feels good. A dear male friend of mine once said, "I want to be good for you, not just good to you." That's some real love right there.

10. Ladies, you were created, by God, to be a helpmate (Genesis 2:18). Scripture literally says that you were made for man (I Corinthians 11:8-9). Therefore, "Happy wife, happy life" and "A man should love you more than you love him" are both unbiblical and selfish. For one thing, as I said in an earlier chapter, aim for healthy over happy instead of making happiness a god, and remember that if your energy is

consumed by trying to be like a man or to outdo one, you are dishonoring the femininity and purpose of it as far as your Creator is concerned. Besides, as one of my favorite quotes says, "If two people were exactly alike, one of them would be unnecessary." (Larry Dixon) True femininity is a spiritual gift and a supernatural power. God doesn't need you to mimic men. Men don't either.

11. There is A LOT of space between "friend" and "enemy". Although our culture may act like it's nothing more than just one big high school, mature folks get that, if you live with intention and character, you tend to have a few true friends and perhaps a few enemies (because if you're being genuine, there is no way that you are everyone's "fit"); however, most folks fall into the "in-between spaces" — and that is just fine, chile. Also, friendships have levels to them. If you believe that you are a temple, then treat your relationships that way: outer court, inner court, most holy. Each layer is earned; they don't "just happen". Also, read up on what Aristotle once said about utility (work), pleasure (play) and good (character) friends. It's also a true relational revelation.

12. Before you state your limits, whatever you're going through with someone may be a misunderstanding. *After* you've articulated your boundaries and they continue to go dismissed, now it's disrespect. You can't be properly loved while being disrespected.

13. Once you become an adult, ANYTHING that you share with others becomes privileged information. I don't care if the individual asking is a relative, a friend, a church leader or anyone else. With adulthood comes privacy. You are the one

who qualifies who is worthy of your inner sanctum of intel —
not them.

14. Mature women don't "live for the fairy tale"; fairy tales are
stories that are told to children; usually make-believe and im-
practical ones, at that (by definition, by the way). Also, "the
princess treatment" doesn't apply to adult relationships. It
can't be said enough that a princess is a father's daughter.
Grown women are queens; a queen is the wife of a king, and
mature relationships come with a lot of responsibilities. By
the way, a king can make a woman a queen, yet a queen can't
make a man a king; just like PRINCE Philip who was married
to QUEEN Elizabeth (some of y'all will catch that later).

15. One of the best movie lines that I've heard in a minute
is, "Real love is liking who you are most around the other
person." Whether it's romantic, familial or platonic, you can
know that you are loved, from a healthy place and space,
when you truly like who you are in their presence — and you
want to become a better version of who you like as well.

16. Originals are incomparable. Problem is, not very many
people live as an original; they are toy soldiers instead, both
in church and out of church. Broad is the way to destruction for the toy soldiers. Narrow is the path for the originals
(Matthew 7:13-14). Choose your path wisely and quit trying
to do what everyone else is doing. A lot of you church folks
are very guilty of that. You aren't original to save your life.
You are carbon copies of folks in the pulpit and the pews.
NOT GOOD.

17. Death is extremely personal between God and his child. You
don't have to understand. God doesn't have to make it make

sense to you. You are finite. He is infinite. His children are his own and their spiritual state is always going to be his biggest priority. At the end of the day, God is the giver of life. What he allows is his right — always has been, always will be. Also, *"The righteous perishes, and no man takes it to heart; merciful men are taken away, while no one considers that the righteous is taken away from evil. He shall enter into peace; they shall rest in their beds, each one walking in his upright-ness."* (Isaiah 57:1-2 — NKJV) Some of y'all need to get into Daniel and Revelation and relearn/unlearn some things. As the Chinese proverb goes, "It's later than you think."

18. If it's not an investment, why are you doing it? Whatever "it" may be. (Investment means "to use, give, or devote (time, talent, etc.), as for a purpose"). These days, I get, more than anything, that if you are giving without it having a purpose behind it, you are actually wasting — time, resources, energy...whatever "it" may be.

19. Love is a gift; not a bribe. 'Nuf said there.

20. CHASE. NOTHING. You were born with your purpose and your dreams come to you. Chasing after something (or one) is a sign that it's the wrong thing or the wrong time — and the right thing at the wrong time *is* the wrong thing.

...

You know, whenever people ask me how I feel about being 50 now, my response is pretty much always the same: "I don't have a problem with aging and 50 ain't old. Now, what *does* trip me out is how fast I went from 30 to 50 and that the next stop is 70. *That* is what's sobering as hell." For real, though.

And yet, to see where I was during my "creative firstborn" known as *Inside of Me* vs. where I am now with my "second child", *Inside of Me 2.0*, I get why "20 "biblically means "patience in waiting" and why hope doesn't just mean that we can have what we want; hope also means that things will turn out for the best, even if what we want doesn't happen when or how we want/wanted it to. The insight, the growth, the shedding and pruning, the confirmations of my purpose — it all has brought me here.

And *this* place? It is good. Actually, y'all, it is RIGHT.

Ultimately, it was all worth it.

Being a student of life, a disciple, always is.

"*As soon as the love relationship does not lead me to me, as soon as I in a love relationship do not lead another person to himself, this love, even if it seems to be the most secure and ecstatic attachment I have ever experienced, is not true love. For real love is dedicated to continual becoming.*"

(LEO BUSCAGLIA)

Aftereffect

Can you tell just how much I adore quotes? Indeed, I do and a writer by the name of Anthony Gucciardi once said, "I have a lot of respect for genuine people. They might not be perfect but at least they are not trying to be." If you add to that the Classic Amplified Version of Luke 12:2, which says, *"Nothing is [so closely] covered up that it will not be revealed, or hidden that it will not be known"* — I think that is how I choose to conclude this offering.

You know, when James 5:16 instructs for us to "confess and be healed", it's not just about telling our stuff as far as revealing our flaws, mistakes and poor decisions — it's also about acknowledging the things that have been revealed to you. Well, as a writer, I have always moved in "genuine confession mode". My mother has cosigned on this before. She once told me that when I was a young child, as we got on a bus, an older woman with a lot of makeup on her face said to me, "You're such a pretty little girl," to which I nonchalantly replied, "And you look like a clown." She also told me that when I was young, if I was off talking to someone by myself, sometimes she would apologize to whomever she was speaking with, to come and see what I was saying because...who knows, chile? Unfortunately, while joking about how much of a "truth speaker" I was then, that ended up turning into forms of ridicule as I got older. There were so many secrets and even flat-out lies swirling around in my space that there was oftentimes more fear than love in my space, which sometimes made me afraid to seek truth — *and speak truth*. Yeah, we have to be careful to not try and turn children into what *we want them to be* (there goes that ego, audacity and narcissism stuff again), and instead, *ask God* how to guide them into who *he called them to become* — because you know what? If something is at their core, if it is genuinely a part of who they are, it's going to come out anyway. I am certainly living proof of that.

And the truth that I stand on now? Now, at 50? It's just what it's defined to be: "the true or actual state of a matter" and "conformity with fact or reality". When John 8:31-32 speaks of the truth setting disciples free, it's not just biblical truth; it's acknowledging what's really going on and accepting the facts and the reality of where we are, not just where we wish things could be.

So, where I am? Oh, I promise you that when *Inside of Me: Lessons of Lust, Love and Redemption* came out in June of 2004 — interestingly enough, the same week that former president Bill Clinton released his own autobiography — I thought that a husband was coming, babies would soon follow, and I probably never would've guessed in a billion years that I would have the firm boundaries that I do or that I wouldn't be a Christian anymore. Yet on this side of life, with *Inside of Me 2.0* being released during the week of Rosh Hashanah of 2024 (which is the new year that I personally observe) and me now being 50, never married, with no children and so far away from the world that I used to know — where I am is at peace with so much wholeness within.

I know my purpose, so I am at peace.

I am a warrior — always have been, always will be — so I am at peace.

I understand what I've been called to do within my bloodline, so I am at peace.

My innermost circle is safe, so I am at peace.

I don't hold on to anything that isn't holding on to me, so I am at peace.

I couldn't care less about the opinions of people who are not invested in my life, so I am at peace.

I know who I am and why I am, so I am at peace and that makes me whole.

Yeah, the beautiful thing about all of this is the Hebrew word for peace, shalom, means things like wholeness, prosperity, good health, well-being, safety, welfare and completion. Yes, I am indeed, "violent" about all of this. In my first book, in many ways, I was fighting against myself because that is how I had damn near been programmed to be. Twenty years later, "perfection in waiting" has taught me to be intentional, aggressive even, about removing and releasing the people, places, things and (perhaps especially) ideas that do not manifest the spirit of shalom into my life. Extreme measures had to be taken in order to get extreme results. At the same time, the funny thing is, it's really only "extreme" to those who don't make peace a top priority in their own life. Time is teaching me that very few actually do.

What's wild is when you start living in this type of head and heart space, when your human trinity — mind, body and spirit — begin to function from a space of total agreement of and for peace, you also learn to make peace: make peace with what you didn't know, make peace with how to reconcile what you didn't know to what you do know now, and make peace with how all of that info will continue to manifest in your life, moving forward.

My life now is not what I thought that it would be like 20 years go — yet oh, in so many ways, it is so much better. Hmph. All of this reminds me of one of my aunts once saying, sarcastically, to me,

"At the rate that you're going, you're never going to get married," to which I simply replied, "That means never divorced too then, right?" And that is something that I am also at peace about: The cost of being a generational curse-breaker can sometimes be quite high. While on one hand, my father will have no one else to continue his bloodline after I am gone, the flip side to this is the nonsense is finally over. I have spoken out about it, I am doing everything in my power to not continue it, and when I leave here, "It is finished." *Literally*. All praises to Adonai. He does all things well.

Listen, I promise you that when I sat down to write this book, I had no idea how it was going to go — yet both books are called *"Inside of Me"* for a reason and, more importantly, a purpose. A lot of sexual brokenness was inside of me back then. A lot of spiritual clarity is inside of me now. Who knows what the next 20 years will bring?

Whatever it is, I have peace about it.

And nothing greater can be said in life, about life, than that.

So let it be written. So let it be done. Again, literally.

Thanks for listening.